CLOUDBURST

More praise for *Cloudburst*

"An outstanding book with the tools you need to be a great fundraiser!"
Cole Wilbur, *Trustee Emeritus and Former President, The David and Lucile Packard Foundation*

"Remarkable! *Cloudburst* showers readers with simple truths that are elusive to so many fundraisers in straightforward and easy to understand language and logic."
Jeffrey Shapiro, *HD PhD, CEO, Edvance Charter Services Group*

"The best book I've read this year and I read three books a week. Brilliant!
Edward Arno, *Managing Director, Pacific Ballet Dance Theater*

"This book is packed with practical tips and techniques; it's an invaluable resource for both new and experienced fundraising professionals."
Jacqueline Parks, *Board Chair of United Way of San Diego County*

"Consider *Cloudburst* your new manifesto for fundraising. This book will completely transform the way you approach fundraising. It's helped me go from scarcity to abundance!"
Olivia Wong, *Social Entrepreneur and Hive Global Leader*

"*Cloudburst* takes the fear out of fundraising! Instead, it becomes a challenge that is fascinating, doable, and life-changing."
Kayla Mertes, *Executive Director, John Corcoran Foundation*

"Lightning strikes twice! You learn how to raise money with confidence and you learn how to keep donors inspired and engaged to give year after year."
Alan Sorkin, *Ex Officio, Social Venture Partners International*

"A win-win! Powerful and instructive insights into both donor and non-profit beliefs and behaviors. Tom has provided a rock solid, valuable, and easily readable resource to the world of philanthropy."
Theo Gund, *Advisory Board Member, Osa Conservation*

CLOUDBURST

*A Rainmaker's Guide
to Fearless Fundraising
and Exceptional Donor Stewardship*

TOM ISELIN

Requests for information or books should be directed to:

Pelican Lake Press
Box 250
Ketchum, ID 83340

Or,

Tom Iselin
First Things First Consulting
www.TomIselin.com
tomiselin@gmail.com
858.888.2278

Report errors in text to: tomiselin@gmail.com.

Discount prices are available for bulk purchases.

Library of Congress Cataloging-in-Publication Data

Iselin, Thomas David, 1961-

> *Cloudburst : A Rainmaker's Guide to Fearless Fundraising and*
> *Exceptional Donor Stewardship*

Tom Iselin: 2nd edition, 4th printing
      p.   cm.

  1. Fundraising   2. Nonprofit Management
  3. Nonprofit Organizations   4. Organizational Development

ISBN: 978-0-9649139-8-1

DEDICATION

To King and Cindy Lambert,
whose love and support never wavers.

~ ~ ~

A portion of the proceeds from the sale of
this book goes to hunger relief organizations.

Thank you for supporting this mission.

Other Books by Tom Iselin:

*First Things First, A Leadership Guide to
Building a Gold Standard Nonprofit*

First Things First – Leadership Guide Workbook

Book discounts available at:

www.TomIselin.com

CONTENTS

FIRST THINGS FIRST
LEARNING CENTER

Would you like to . . .

Raise more money and improve your fundraising skills?

Kick-start a major donor giving program?

Learn winning solicitation tactics?

Build your confidence to handle objections?

Learn the subtleties of stewarding donors?

Watch training videos that cover key principles and tactics of this book?

Create a *get it done!* board and staff culture?

Avoid common mistakes that lead to organizational dysfunction?

Build a "gold standard" nonprofit that's the envy of others?

If you said "Yes," then visit TomIselin.com and become a fan, or visit one of his social media sites and become a subscriber. You'll receive notices for all types of useful tools that will help you improve your fundraising skills, build a thriving nonprofit, and live inspired.

- Entertaining "how-to" video tutorials
- Role-playing videos
- Video blog
- Podcasts (iTunes: "Tom Iselin")
- YouTube, Facebook, Instagram ("Tom Iselin")
- Interviews with industry experts
- Articles and information
- Books and workbooks

This book is a sequel to *First Things First, A Leadership Guide to Building a Gold Standard Nonprofit.* To buy copies of these books and others, visit the website.

www.TomIselin.com

THE AUTHOR

Asking for money has always been a way of life for Tom. In junior high, he asked neighbors if he could mow lawns and shovel snow for spending money. In high school, he went door-to-door selling Kirby vacuum cleaners, and in college, he made cold calls to company executives to sell refurbished mainframe computers.

In the 1980s, Tom became a stock options trader on the floor of the Chicago Mercantile Exchange, where he learned the art of negotiating prices quickly, precisely, and confidently in turbulent settings.

After a near-death experience in 1991, Tom hung up his trading jacket and became a social entrepreneur. He went on to help build some of the sector's most notable nonprofits such as Natural High, Sun Valley Adaptive Sports, Kids First Foundation, and the Environmental News Network. He also founded The Hunger Coalition and one of the nation's largest and most innovative sports rehabilitation programs for veterans and wounded warriors called Higher Ground.

Part of Tom's success in building high-performance nonprofits was his uncanny ability to raise money. Known as "The Rainmaker," Tom's secret to raising money was building relationships with donors and then asking them for money in face-to-face settings.

This simple approach to fundraising helped Tom raise tens of millions of dollars and it's the same approach he has shared with thousands of nonprofits to help them raise hundreds of millions of dollars.

Hailed as "One of the most inspiring speakers you'll ever hear," you'll find Tom traveling around the country teaching workshops and speaking at conferences to share his passions in an effort to transform nervous staff and board members into thundering Rainmakers, helping them to raise money and ask for favors with confidence and ease.

This is Tom's sixth book. He runs a consulting business and lives in Sun Valley, ID. To relax, Tom likes to play tennis, fly fish, and ride his mountain bike. He also likes to cook, bake, and hike the Swiss Alps.

ACKNOWLEDGMENTS

Sincere thanks to Kim Mason, Phyllis Sarkana, and Kathleen Turner, my star editors, and to all my friends and family who provided thoughtful input and scoured the text looking for typos: Chris Yanov, Brigit Cavanagh, Celia Giacobbi, Cynthia Breunig, Kayla Scheidler, Denise Jones, Gigi Trebatoski, Juliet Hutchens, Jacqueline Parks, Paula Isley, Jeannette Davidson-Mayer, Michael Spitters, Olivia Wong, Sam Brooks, Lindsay Stryker, and Theo Gund.

I also want to extend a special thanks to Tim Mantoani who shot the photograph on the back cover, and to Kari Young for the amazing work she did on the cover design.

Most of all, I want to thank my sweetheart, Sara. Her heart is made of gold and I'm forever indebted to her enduring love, continued support, and generous encouragement of my work to help others.

* * * * *

There are a lot of smart Rainmakers out there and I want to thank a few of my peers who have a passion to help people and shape a constantly evolving industry. These folks write books and blogs, host workshops and webinars, and speak at conferences around the country. I've gleaned a lifetime of insights from these masters and have adopted variations of their material into my own, some of which are in *Cloudburst*.

If you get a chance to read their material or see them speak, you're in for a treat: Jerold Panas, Ken Burnett, Laura Fredricks, Rodger Craver, Beverly Browning, Stuart Wilde, Jeffrey Fox, Douglass Alexander, Kristina Carlson, Russell Granger, Bernard Ross, Clare Segal, Adrian Sargeant, Tom Ahern, and Elaine Jay.

* * * * *

A note on terminology
Throughout the book, I use the term "major donor" to mean the same thing as what others refer to as a "high-level donor" or "high-value donor." I also use the term "minor donor" to mean the same thing as what others refer to as a "low-level donor" or "low-value donor."

INTRODUCTION

Competition for funding is fierce. You and more than a million charities are duking it out for a limited pool of funding. Without funding, your mission will flounder. You must raise money. Failure is not an option.

That's enough pressure to make anyone anxious about fundraising. Whatever your role, whatever your experience, and whatever the reason you're helping raise money for your nonprofit, *Cloudburst* gives you the tools you need and the mindset required to improve your skills to wisely and fearlessly ask for money in face-to-face settings.

The book offers dozens of tactics and examples to help you learn the subtleties of asking for money and overcoming objections. But just as important as getting checks is, you'll learn the art of cultivating donors before they give, and stewarding donors after they give, allowing you to transform one-time givers into loyal and involved donors who are thrilled to support you year after year.

Cloudburst provides straight talk that makes sense. There are no long-winded stories, no highbrow theories, and no confusing statistics. It's a comprehensive how-to book, but its principles and tactics are easy to understand and apply. I repeat key concepts throughout the book to help you learn them, and I designed chapters as stand-alone segments so you can refer to specific tactics when you need a refresher.

For 20 years, I honed a set of fundraising strategies that helped me raise tens of millions of dollars and I've been sharing them with thousands of nonprofits to help them raise hundreds of millions of dollars.

Now it's your turn. *Cloudburst* will show you how to become a *Rainmaker,* an expert at raising money the way donors expect you to raise money, and the way that motivates them to be loyal, generous, longtime donors.

Good fortune floats in the clouds above you. Are you ready to burst these clouds and make it rain money so your mission can flourish? Raising money may not be an option, but it is an opportunity. Let me show you how to embrace it with confidence and passion.

CHAPTER 1

FUNDRAISING FACTS

Number of US charities and foundations

Charities   958,740
Foundations   98,746
Source: The Urban Institute

Sources of charitable giving

Individuals   81% $241.9 billion
Foundations   14% $41.67 billion
Corporations   5% $14.55 billion
Source: Giving USA

How much does the government give to charities?

$137 billion, the bulk of which goes to education, health care, and cultural institutions.
Source: The Urban Institute

Most charities are small with limited resources

80% of charities have budgets less than $500,000.
90% of charities have budgets less than $2 million.
20% of all donations go to the top 400 charities. (Read that again!)
Source: The Urban Institute

Households

Number of Americans that make more the $100,000 a year: 15 million.
U.S. households with a net worth of $1 million or more: 1,000,000.
Donors above age 65 account for 46 percent of all giving.
Donors below age 35 account for just 4 percent of all giving.
Source: Chronicle of Philanthropy

I want to make a difference with my money

75 percent of donors say "a willingness to make a difference" motivates them to give.
Source: First Things First market analysis

I want to make a difference with my money after I'm gone

60 percent of wealthy people plan to leave money to a charity after they die. Most legacy gifts come from estates worth $2.0 million or less.
Source: Chronicle of Philanthropy

Ask me in person

More than 70 percent of people will say "Yes" to a face-to-face ask if they have an emotional connection to a nonprofit. This figure can jump to 90 percent if they faithfully volunteer and the ask is made at a location where the nonprofit's programming is taking place.
Source: First Things First market analysis

Let's have lunch

Conducting an ask in a face-to-face setting is 20 times more effective than sending an appeal letter in the mail.
Source: Adrian Sargeant, Building Donor Loyalty

Replacing me is expensive

It costs five times more to acquire a new donor than to reactivate a lapsed donor and 10 times more than to keep in touch with an existing donor.
Source: Adrian Sargeant, Building Donor Loyalty

The longer I'm around, the more I'm worth

There is a 70-80 percent chance donors will stop giving after they make their first gift and a 30 percent chance every year after that. A mere 10 percent reduction in donor attrition can lead to a 100 percent increase in the lifetime value of donors over 10 years.
Source: Adrian Sargeant, Building Donor Loyalty

The more I'm involved, the more I'm worth

Donors who volunteer donate nearly 50 percent more money than they did before they started volunteering. When they help, they offer time, provide expertise, make referrals, attend events, become ambassadors, and make in-kind gifts. The total lifetime value of loyal, involved donors can be 10, 50, or 100 times the value of their financial gifts.
Source: First Things First market analysis

If I have a bad experience with you, I'll tell my friends

More than 90 percent of donors who have a beef with you won't tell you, but they will tell at least seven of their friends.
Source: Adrian Sargeant, Building Donor Loyalty

I like to give during the holidays

On average, donors make 30 percent of their annual contributions between Thanksgiving and New Year's.
Source: Center on Philanthropy

CHAPTER 2

PLAY THE ODDS

The 10 most effective communication methods used to raise money:

1. One-on-one meetings
2. Small group meetings or parties
3. Telephone conversations
4. Personalized handwritten letters
5. Personalized typed letters
6. Email or text solicitation (those with videos and pics do better)
7. Web, blog, and video solicitation (gaining momentum)
8. Galas or large group events
9. Direct mail solicitation (no personalization)
10. Grants

Notice the top two methods center on talking with people in *face-to-face settings*. Now, get this . . . 80 percent of all money given to nonprofits comes from individuals and 80 percent of this money comes from wealthy donors who were asked using the top two methods above, plus #8.

What does this tell you? It tells you that you should be spending more time building relationships with donors, especially wealthy donors, and asking them for money in face-to-face settings. How much time? Up to 50 percent depending on your capacity and your ability to raise money from other income channels.

Some nonprofits spend as little as five percent of their time raising money in this manner. Instead, they spend hundreds of hours writing small grants and thousands of hours organizing low-yield galas. The result? Frustration and low dollar-per-hour fundraising results.

Sound familiar? Writing grants and hosting galas can be effective means of raising money, but Rainmakers play the odds. They write grants and host galas, but they know the best return per hour is spent building and managing relationships with donors, especially major (high-level) donors, and raising money from them in face-to-face settings. This is the most important principle in this book and the essence of Rainmaker magic.

CHAPTER 3
SHOULD *YOU* BE ASKING FOR MONEY?

One of the worst mistakes a nonprofit can make is requiring people to ask for money. When a person feels pressured to ask for money or favors, or is afraid to ask, or loathes the task, bad things can happen:

1. A missed donation because the asker was ineffective

2. A smaller donation because the asker was ineffective

3. A donor leaves the nonprofit due to a bad experience

4. A donor tells other donors and friends of their bad experience

5. The asker leaves the nonprofit because they feel forced to ask for money, or they feel uncomfortable asking for money

What does this mean for you? It means if you're not genuinely excited and passionate about asking people for money, you shouldn't be doing it. Let someone else do it. If you are interested in asking donors for money but are terrible at it, or nervous about it, or would like to get better at it, you can learn to be an effective asker.

Now, if you're a board member, your fear of asking for money or lack of skill to do it doesn't let you off the fundraising hook. It's your responsibility to *support* the fundraising efforts of your nonprofit to ensure it can meet its financial obligations. There are plenty of ways to do this that don't involve asking people for money, as you'll learn in the following sections.

Gut check: If you're a board member and unwilling to support the fundraising efforts of the nonprofit you care so much about, you should think seriously about stepping aside and taking on a role that doesn't involve fundraising. You could be a committee member, advisory board member, or a volunteer. This way you can still contribute to your nonprofit without feeling obligated to support its fundraising efforts. Think about it. Do the right thing.

CHAPTER 4

BUILDING A
RAINMAKER TEAM

A successful fundraising program requires a *team*. A nonprofit that places all its fundraising responsibilities on the back of one person is set up for failure. There will not be enough capacity to do an outstanding job, and it's risky; what if the person suddenly leaves?

An effective program requires an adequate supply of rainmaking capacity (human, financial, technological, marketing) to achieve its objectives. Rainmakers know the most important type of capacity is human capital: board members, staff, volunteers, and donors.

This means there are no hall passes—everyone on the team must play a role. Not everyone has to ask for money, but everyone has skills and time to contribute that the team can use to achieve its objectives.

Exercise

What follows are profile descriptions of the six types of people you'll need to build a winning fundraising team. Use them to categorize the types of people you already have on your team, take inventory of the team's strengths and weaknesses, and make changes that will improve the composition of the team, including the option of adding new members.

On a whiteboard, draw a large-scale version of the matrix on page 18. Make photocopies of the following fundraising profiles and have team members read them. Then have each member rank their top three profile categories based on interest and in order of preference, "1" being their top choice. Plot each member's responses on the whiteboard.

Most teams that go through this exercise discover they have an abundance of champions, supporters, and hosts, and a shortage of leaders, connectors, and askers. If your team finds itself in this position, it may want to find additional members with specific skill sets, or ask current members to take on different positions, which may require training and coaching.

Leaders

These people have fundraising expertise. They understand the big picture and key principles and processes that need to be in place for a fundraising plan to succeed. They know how to lead and inspire people to accomplish the tasks at hand. Many leaders are talented Rainmakers and make great mentors.

Champions

These people are enthusiastic ambassadors. They love the stage and enjoy telling compelling stories to get people excited and engaged about the work you're doing and why they should get involved. With a little training, champions can become great askers because of their public speaking ability and confidence.

Connectors

These people know people. They have valuable networks of friends and business associates. If they don't have a direct connection to a person you'd like to reach, they are only a phone call away from someone who does. This is a good role for major donors and busy CEOs.

Hosts

These people like to host events or help organize them. They have the gift of hospitality. They love to decorate, cook, and mingle. They enjoy managing the details of events to make them memorable.

Askers

These people are willing to ask people for anything—money, in-kind gifts, and favors. They are confident, likeable, engaging, and interesting. They know how to craft an ask that inspires donors to joyfully say "Yes." They understand donor stewardship is the key to long-term fundraising success and they are good at it.

Supporters

These people are the unsung heroes of a fundraising team. They provide crucial "back office" support that keeps the entire fundraising process flowing smoothly: marketing, follow up, event planning, and administrative duties. They are willing to roll up their sleeves and do tedious work few people ever see, such as cleaning up after an event, licking envelopes, and updating donor profiles in a database.

Rainmaker Team Profile
(Example)

	Leader	Champion	Connector	Host	Asker	Supporter
Name						
Sara	1		2			3
Jenny		1	3	2		
Malcom		1		2		3
Wendell		3		1		2
Myra	3	1				2
Anahid		2		3	1	
Sophia			1	2		3
Patrick		3		1		2
Barry		1	3		2	

As you can see in this example, there is an abundance of interest in the Champions category, but little in the Asker category. This is common among fundraising teams. To become a Rainmaker team, this team would want to rebalance its profile makeup by asking some of its Champions to become Askers, in addition to being Champions.

With so much interest in the Host and Supporter categories, this team should consider hosting a series of small dinner parties or fundraising events, where the Hosts can dazzle donors with their gifts of hospitality and the Supporters can help manage all the details.

Finally, they will want to add more Leaders and Connecters to their team to broaden the collective expertise of the team. More Leaders mean more fundraising knowledge, experience, and inspiration. More Connectors mean more donors, partnerships, and influence in the community.

What is the profile makeup of your fundraising team? How could you rebalance it to improve the effectiveness of your fundraising efforts?

"There are no hall passes.
Everyone responsible for raising money
must play a role."

CHAPTER 5
HELP RAISE MONEY
WITHOUT ASKING FOR IT

As you learned in the last chapter, there are many ways your team members can act as Rainmakers without ever having to ask someone for money. What's most important is that all team members roll up their sleeves, get involved, and use their time, expertise, and influence to help support the fundraising efforts of your nonprofit.

Exercise

Create an "engagement form" from the choices below and ask team members to choose the fundraising tasks that interest them. Then have your team use the results to engage team members based on their interests, level of competency, and time availability.

❑ Public speaking
❑ Host a dinner/event
❑ Make introductions
❑ Work on the fundraising plan
❑ Write thank-you letters
❑ Write email/mail solicitations
❑ Chair a major event
❑ Identify government agencies
❑ Network with donors at events
❑ Help with administrative duties
❑ Gala/event preparation
❑ Donor cultivation and stewardship
❑ Find event sponsors
❑ Give facility tours
❑ Make thank-you phone calls
❑ Grant writing/reporting
❑ Marketing/promotion/PR
❑ Database entry
❑ Secure in-kind gifts
❑ Write appeal letters
❑ Negotiate reduced pricing/fees from vendors
❑ Identify donors, corporations, foundations
❑ Work with city officials to secure permits

Let's assume your Rainmaker team is in place and everyone has chosen ways to support the fundraising efforts of your organization. Great! Now it's time to learn about donors and what influences their decisions about nonprofits and giving.

CHAPTER 6

THE SUPER 6

There are many factors (reasons and motives) that influence a donor's decision when selecting a nonprofit to support. However, six of these consistently stand head-and-shoulders above the rest. Rainmakers call these factors "The Super 6" because the higher a donor emotionally and mentally rates a nonprofit on these six factors, the greater the likelihood the nonprofit will receive money.

You should always be thinking about how your donors are rating you in each category, and you should always be trying to find ways to improve your Super 6 score.

The Super 6
Factors that influence a donor's decision to
select a nonprofit to support:

1. Issues they care about

2. Missions they believe in

3. Organizations they trust

4. People they like

5. First-rate performance and impact

6. Outstanding donor relations and customer service

1. Issues they care about
If a donor doesn't care about antique art restoration, it's unlikely they will support a nonprofit whose mission it is to restore antique art. Sure, they may make a small, one-time gift if a friend asks them to make a donation, but they're unlikely to become an engaged, longtime donor.

However, if a donor cares about antique art restoration, then the donor may be receptive to supporting a number of nonprofits that address the issue of antique art restoration.

Find and retain more donors who care about the issue you're addressing. Or, spend time to educate and convince potential donors why they *should* care about the issue.

2. Missions they believe in
In larger cities there might be a dozen different missions addressing a single issue (e.g., hunger). When faced with a variety of mission choices to address an issue, a donor will typically choose a mission they *believe* in.

For example, one donor may believe strongly in supporting soup kitchens, while another may believe strongly in supporting Meals on Wheels programs for seniors.

Once you find donors who care about your issue, you'll need to show them how your mission distinguishes itself from the other missions addressing the same issue. Some donors support multiple missions that address an issue, but most donors choose only one mission addressing an issue. Why should donors support your mission and not the one across town?

3. Organizations they trust
Donors like to support nonprofits they trust. They want to feel secure that the nonprofits they give money to are trustworthy and will use their money wisely.

They expect reliable service and consistent messages. They expect you to run a professional organization with the highest ethical standards. If you can't do these things, or donors *feel* you can't do these things, you'll lose credibility. If you lose credibility, say "bye-bye" to your donors.

4. People they like
People like to do business with people they like. If you want to win the generosity of donors, you need to be personable and develop friendly, professional relationships with donors. Spend time with donors *in person*. Get to know them as you would a neighbor or a coworker. Learn about their interests and families. For smaller donors, spend time with them on social media.

You can have the highest performing programming in your sector, but your fundraising efforts will flop if the people you have asking for money are dull, grumpy, rude, or unreliable. Or worse yet, you force or coerce people to ask for money.

The people you choose to raise money will have a direct impact on your nonprofit's ability to raise money and build an outstanding fundraising program—so choose wisely.

Forget about age and business background. Select people who *want* to raise money. Select people who are passionate, personable, interesting, honest, and reliable. Select people who know how to make others feel good, generously give thanks and express gratitude, and know how to inspire others and get them involved.

5. First-rate performance and impact

Donors have choices and they like to pick winners. They want to know their "social investments" are making a difference. Why should they choose you? What are you doing to prove to donors that you're a high-performance nonprofit worthy of their support?

The nonprofit world is fiercely competitive. To win the loyalty of donors, you need to show them, on a regular basis, and in a compelling fashion, the short-term and long-term impact your work is having on the people you serve, your community, and the issue you're addressing.

Show donors that you have effective management, use funds wisely, and run well-organized programs. Show them you have engaged board members, competent staff, and a strong brand. Show them the lives you're changing, and show them you have an inspiring vision and a sound plan to achieve it.

Remember, it's more impressive to show how *deep* you are than how big you are, or how fast you're growing.

6. Outstanding donor relations and customer service

One of the leading reasons why donors make a first gift and subsequent gifts is based on how they are treated. If you want to acquire and retain more donors, institute a systematic process to nurture relationships with donors from the time you meet them to the time they stop donating (and sometimes longer), regardless of their level of giving.

For major donors, set up a process to talk with them on the phone, meet them for coffee or lunch, or invite them to a special event. For smaller donors, it may be good enough to nurture relationships through email, text messages, and social media. For all donors, invite them to outreach events and galas, keep them informed, involve them in volunteer work, and do little things that make them feel valued, appreciated, and happy.

Whatever you do to nurture relationships with donors, make sure it's consistent, meaningful, and personalized. Remember, if your "touch" with donors grows cold, their gifts will grow cold too.

It's also important to keep in mind your nonprofit is in the customer service business. Think of your donors as customers. They pay you to deliver programs and services, and they expect to be treated with respect and gratitude for supporting you.

Each time a donor calls your office, requests information, or bumps into you in the street, they are giving you a customer service score. What customer service score would each of the donors you manage give you? What customer service score would they give your nonprofit?

If you want to win the loyalty of donors, show them you care. Greet them warmly, respond to requests promptly, keep them informed, empathize with their position, listen to their feedback, and go the extra mile. Think "Concierge Service" and make the experience for the donor—in every situation—unexpectedly pleasurable.

Exercise:
Create an online survey where donors can rate their donor experience in each of The Super 6 categories. Create a 1 to 10 rating system and limit the survey only to The Super 6 categories. Assure donors that the survey is confidential and encourage them to be candid. The results may shock you—but they will also help you.

"It's more impressive to show how *deep* you are
than how big you are,
or how fast you're growing."

CHAPTER 7

THE BIG 2

Rainmakers use The Super 6 to understand the primary decision-making factors donors use to *select* a nonprofit to support. Once donors start giving, there are dozens of factors that influence their willingness to *continue* giving, including the Super 6.

The following chapters cover many of these decision-making factors in detail, but Rainmakers know the most powerful factors that determine continued giving are based on responses donors give to two questions ("The Big 2") they ask themselves, either consciously or subconsciously.

The Big 2

Factors that influence a donor's decision to
continue giving to a nonprofit:

1. Has my donation made a difference and will it continue to make a difference?

2. Do I feel valued and appreciated for all the monetary and non-monetary contributions I've made?

That's it. If you continually show donors their contributions are making a difference and they feel valued and appreciated for their contributions, you'll have little trouble raising the money you need to fulfill your mission and achieve your dreams.

Okay, it's a bit more involved than that, but these are two "big" steps in the right direction.

"Call a donor just to say 'Hi!'
More than 60 percent of nonprofits
call donors only to ask for money."

CHAPTER 8
SWEAT THE THINGS YOU CAN CONTROL

The willingness of a donor to make a gift, and the size and frequency of their gift, may have nothing to do with you and your nonprofit and everything to do with their circumstances.

They may give less because they're going through a divorce or job change. They may delay giving because they're having surgery, buying a house, or paying tuition bills. Or, they may stop giving because they're moving out of state or feeling depressed.

Rainmakers don't sweat the stuff they can't control. If you have a donor facing adversity or change, express empathy and grace, and exercise patience. Ask the donor how they would like to be kept informed and remain connected. Keep the pressure off and turn the compassion on.

Sweat the things you can control
On the other hand, the size, frequency, and willingness of a donor to make a gift may have nothing to do with a donor's circumstances and everything to do with you and your nonprofit.

A donor may give less because you're unreliable and did not explain how their gift is making a difference. They may delay giving because they're annoyed with all the emails you're sending, or because no one has expressed appreciation for their volunteer work. They may stop giving because you didn't thank them, or they felt used.

Rainmakers do sweat the stuff they *can* control. This is why it's imperative that you strive to improve operational performance, donor relations, and customer service. You must show donors that their money is making a difference and that you care about them. You want the entire donor experience to be exceptional because happy, satisfied donors make loyal, generous donors. The small stuff matters—do more of it.

CHAPTER 9

10 STRATEGIC FUNDRAISING PRINCIPLES

When raising money in face-to-face settings, Rainmakers keep things simple. They focus on what they can control and build their fundraising strategies and tactics around the following nine principles to increase their chances of fundraising success.

1. Build sticky relationships

2. Make a "connection ask" first

3. Increase the number of face-to-face asks

4. Find and keep more donors

5. Get donors involved

6. Personalize and customize everything

7. Just ask!

8. Focus on the needs you fill

9. Change your pronouns . . . use more "You"

10.Create more goose bumps

1. Build sticky relationships

Why? Future donations are directly related to the quality of relationships you develop with donors. How would you feel if you donated $5,000 to a cause you cared about and the next call you received from the nonprofit was *a year later* asking for another $5,000?

No one wants to feel like a cash machine. If there is no relationship between the asker and donor, and the donor is ignored, you will lose the donor. Period.

Rainmakers know relationships create trust, credibility, and stickiness that keep donors loyal. If you want to create more loyal and generous donors, make more meaningful, personalized connections with them and do the small stuff that makes them feel good about you and your nonprofit.

Get to know your donors as people. Learn about their interests, work, families, background, and philanthropic interests. If you invest the time and genuinely get to know your donors in a friendly but professional manner, they will "stick" around.

2. Make a "connection ask" first

It can be very difficult to get donors to give money if you have no relationship with them and they have little to no connection to your nonprofit.

This is why Rainmakers typically make their first ask a non-monetary ask—a "connection ask." Instead of asking for money, ask donors to observe your programming, volunteer for a day, take a site tour, watch a performance, or attend a "friend-raising" event.

This approach removes the pressure of having to ask for money. Instead, it ignites interest, emotionally connects donors to the good work you're doing, and starts a relationship. After doing this a few times, donors will be much more receptive to making a donation. You can also apply this principle to longtime donors as you prepare to ask them for donations. Also see "Non-monetary Ask" on page 92.

3. Increase the number of face-to-face asks

Asking for money in face-to-face settings is the most effective tactic you can use to raise money, especially from major donors. However, some nonprofits spend less than five percent of their total fundraising efforts on face-to-face asks.

Not Rainmakers. They spend up to 50 percent of their time raising money in face-to-face settings. You should do the same because it gives you a chance to connect with donors, nurture relationships, build trust, explain the work of your nonprofit in detail, express your passion for the mission, and ask donors directly for a donation.

Pick up the phone and call your donors. Take them out for coffee or lunch. Invite them to a small dinner party or to an event. Unless you have a specific reason to do otherwise, *always* ask major donors, and select medium-sized donors, for money in person. It's okay to use other methods to ask for money from these types of donors; just make face-to-face asking your primary method.

Try this: In the next year, triple the amount of time you spend in face-to-face meetings with donors and see what the results bring.

4. Find and keep more donors

It takes 200 people each making $100 donations to equal just one $20,000 donation. It can take dozens of hours to manage 200 donors throughout the year, but it may take only 10 hours a year to manage one $20,000 donor.

Rainmakers know that time and resources are in short supply so they are constantly trying to acquire and retain more donors, with an emphasis on major donors.

Yes, it's challenging to find even a few $5,000, $10,000, and $20,000 donors each year, but it's worth it. Create systems to get referrals from board members, volunteers, staff, and other donors. Speak at corporations and civic organizations. Get more radio and television time. Use social media.

But wait! What good is it if you land a major donor, only to lose them after one year? Donors leave for many reasons, but you don't want them to leave because you neglected them. Remember, it costs five times more to acquire a new donor than to reactivate a lapsed donor, and 10 times more than to keep in touch with an existing donor. To retain the donors you land, you need to create detailed stewardship programs to keep your donors happy and engaged.

What about minor donors?
Rainmakers always want more major donors, but they know the value of having more donors of any size. They know the more donors you have, the greater the potential you have to raise more money and the greater the chance a few minor donors might turn into a few major donors.

Plus, every time you fold in a new donor of any size, you increase the potential of unforeseen benefits. Donors can become powerful ambassadors, contribute expertise, connect you to influential people, and become star volunteers. Therefore, more donors mean more potential value!

Try this: Make a goal to increase your donor base by 20 percent a year. To build your list of donors, ask for referrals from board members, staff, donors, and volunteers. You should also solicit donors online, give tours, and host friend-raisers, open houses, and awareness events.

5. Get donors involved

When donors roll up their sleeves and get involved with the work of a nonprofit, or touch its magic in some way, they get emotionally connected, which deepens their passion about the mission and increases the chances of support.

Rainmakers work hard to involve donors because they know engaged donors make loyal, generous donors and faithful fans. Involved do nors are also more likely to provide unforeseen benefits such as business contacts, office space, political influence, introductions to friends, and in-kind gifts.

There are many levels of involvement. Some may require little commitment, such as observing a program, attending a social function, or sponsoring a table at a special event. Others may require extensive commitments such as joining a committee, hosting a dinner party, solving a problem, or volunteering for a program.

Try this: To determine the interests of your donors, ask them to complete a "donor engagement form." The form should have a series of checkboxes outlining ways donors can get involved. Keep it simple. Offer a variety of options, and include a few open-ended questions asking donors about their skills, interest, experience, and availability.

6. Personalize and customize everything

The more special you make a donor feel, the more goodwill deposits you make. The more deposits you make, the more likely a donor will say "Yes" when you ask for a withdrawal (donation).

Rainmakers know that the larger the donor, the more personalized attention you should give them. Make them feel like they are your most loyal and valued donor—your *only* donor. Whether you're writing an ask letter, making a phone call, or meeting a major donor for lunch, try to personalize and customize everything you say and do.

Try this: Handwrite invitations, thank-you notes, and envelope addresses. Write thoughtful inscriptions at the bottom of annual reports, appeal letters, and on the outside of envelopes. Create a custom video for a donor or send a custom photo album that shows them interacting with your beneficiaries. Whatever you do, make it professional and classy. Nothing gaudy.

7. Just Ask!

There is a 70 percent chance people will say "Yes" to a face-to-face ask if they have an emotional connection to a nonprofit. This percentage can top 90 percent if they are faithful volunteers and the ask is made in a setting where the nonprofit's programming is taking place.

Rainmakers know these are incredible statistics, which is why they spend so much time building relationships with donors, getting them involved, and then asking them for money in settings where the probability of a "Yes" is the greatest.

You'll hear it again and again; no other fundraising principle is more important. It's a Rainmaker's secret sauce. Start making a batch today!

8. Focus on the needs you fill

One of the biggest mistakes fundraisers make when asking for money is focusing on the needs of their nonprofits: "*We* need money to add staff." "*We* need money to buy a new building." This type of positioning tells the donor of *your* needs.

Rainmakers don't make this mistake. When they ask for money, they frame the ask to show how their beneficiaries will benefit from receiving the money, not how their nonprofits will benefit.

Instead of saying, "We need money to buy laptops to help students learn," say, "Grades of children increase 20 percent when they have their own laptops. They also take 15 percent more honors classes and have a 40 percent higher matriculation rate into college. Your gift of $5,000 will buy 25 children their own laptops."

9. Change your pronouns . . . use more "You"

Grab a couple of your recently written appeal letters, thank-you notes, and newsletters. Circle every instance of the pronouns "us," "we," "our," "I," and "me." Now put a square around every instance of the pronouns "you," "your," "you're," "you've," and every use of the form "donor." The results will probably startle you. The writing of most nonprofits is very self-centered, almost narcissistic. Their copy is all about the great work *they've* done or will do. They yarn about all *their* programs, jabber about *their* board members, and ramble about the change *they* made in the lives of the kids they serve. It's EGO writing.

As Tom Ahern says, "'YOU' is glue! It will raise oceans of money. Those who use 'you' well, do well." Start writing donor centric copy. Make the donor the hero. Flatter them. Love them. Thank them. And do it over and over again. "Without your help . . ." "Your support saved . . ." "Because of you . . ." "You made a difference . . ."

10. Create more goose bumps

There are more than a million charities competing for a limited amount of funding and resources. If you want your share, you need to stand out and speak loudly. Otherwise, you will end up in the "heap of the unknowns" with thousands of other nonprofits that are doing great work but remain penniless because too few people know who they are, what they do, and the impact they're having. Rainmakers know the backbone of great fundraising is savvy marketing. They know that positive public images, clear messaging, and top-of-mind association are keys to inspiring and motivating donors to give money and get involved.

Quality marketing will require you to create compelling stories, powerful collateral, stunning videos, and striking images that give people goose bumps. To do this, you'll need to build a quiver of high quality marketing collateral (Chapter 34). To produce these items, you'll need a team of people who are highly skilled in the areas of promotion, publicity, graphic design, branding, photography, and videography.

This is a tall order, indeed. However, there is hope. If you don't have a marketing staff or a large marketing budget, then outsource the work. Look to local businesses, public relations firms, advertising agencies, universities, and freelancers. You may find a person or a small team willing to discount their services, or perhaps provide them for free.

The work you're doing is too important for people not to see and hear about it, but it's essential you share it in a way that makes it exciting and unforgettable.

CHAPTER 10

HOW TO BE A HIT
IN 60 SECONDS

Your nonprofit may be best in class, but you'll be hard pressed to raise a dime from donors if they dislike you. It all starts with first impressions. When you meet a donor for the first time, they will make a judgment about you in less than a minute.

This impression may be so strong that it becomes indelible and, for better or worse, forever affects how they feel about you and their willingness to give to your cause.

Rainmakers know that you only get one chance to make a first impression. Here are five simple tactics you can use to help make your first impressions amazing ones.

Be a Hit in 60 Seconds

1. Arrive on time!

2. Greet donors with a friendly smile and firm handshake

3. Express an energized spirit and positive attitude

4. Maintain warm and constant eye contact

5. Have good hygiene and smell neutral

1. Arrive on time!
If you're not early, you're late! Many donors, especially business types, have high standards when it comes to punctuality. Rainmakers know that you may not win brownie points for showing up early, but showing up late may leave an impression that tastes like burnt garlic.

Arrive at meetings 10-15 minutes early. With your spare time, sit in your car, relax, and think about how you'd like the meeting to unfold. If you're meeting at a restaurant, go in and pick out the perfect table. Always plan for traffic delays and getting lost. Be smart and plan for the unexpected.

2. Greet donors with a friendly smile and firm handshake

Friendly personalities attract donors. It makes them feel safe and comfortable. Rainmakers greet donors as if they're meeting a friend that they haven't seen in a while. The warmth you share through a friendly smile and firm handshake may be all you need to win a donor's heart.

3. Express an energized spirit and positive attitude

Rainmakers are acutely aware that what they say, how they say it, and their body language are all sending signals to a donor. They each get rated as positive, neutral, or negative. You've been given a ticket to the big game! Bring your enthusiasm and be prepared to share the excitement of why you're such a big fan of your mission.

4. Maintain warm and constant eye contact

As the adage goes, "Your eyes are the windows to your soul." In a few seconds, a donor can peer into your eyes and tell whether you're happy or sad, tired or excited, confident or fearful, distracted, or engaged. When talking with a donor, Rainmakers maintain comfortable eye contact and consciously express their delight and interest in donors and the moment.

5. Have good hygiene and smell neutral

The aroma of our perfume or cologne can be repulsive to some people. Rainmakers know that bad breath, dirty fingernails, poor grooming, and sloppy clothes can be big turnoffs. Make a sparkling impression by showing up polished and smelling neutral.

"A note on meetings:
If you're not early, you're late!"

CHAPTER 11

7 WAYS TO MAKE YOURSELF MEMORABLE

It's important you make a good first impression, but Rainmakers know it's even more important to make a lasting impression if they expect donors to remain happy and generous. To make a lasting impression, you need to *consistently* do the small stuff that will make you memorable. Here are seven tactics you can use that will help you stand out like a shining star in a donor's mind.

Make Yourself Memorable

1. Express honesty, humility, and candor

2. Follow through every time

3. Show donors you value and appreciate them

4. Know your stuff

5. Talk less, listen more, and ask interesting questions

6. Express your passion

7. Live an inspired life and develop your own interests

1. Express honesty, humility, and candor

Donors respect and admire honest and humble people. They see plenty of big egos in their own world. If you want to quickly lose the attention of a donor, just brag. If you want donors to be your fans, be candid and gracious in their presence and thank them for all the kind things they do for you, your nonprofit, and the community.

2. Follow through every time

Donors do not want to second-guess. They expect reliability. They respect a strong work ethic. Do you show up on time? Do you follow up when you say you will? Can donors count on you? Show donors you're dependable by exceeding expectations on the tasks they expect you to deliver.

3. Show donors you value and appreciate them

Treat donors like cash machines and you'll soon find a "closed for business" sign hanging on their front doors. Show donors you value and appreciate them for who they are, not just for the gifts they provide. Keep it simple. Make it sincere.

Send a *handwritten* note telling them how grateful you are for their friendship, make them dinner, or ask them to join you for an evening of wine tasting. Treat them like a partner and make them feel like they are part of the solution to fulfilling your mission. Expressing your gratitude will be repaid with loyalty and generosity.

4. Know your stuff

Donors want to work with credible people and support credible nonprofits. Donors will ask many types of questions about your nonprofit and they expect you'll have the answers to most of them. The more you know, the more credible you'll sound and the more confident donors will feel that they are working with someone they trust and respect, which equates to more gifts and happy donors.

Learn how to answer basic questions about your nonprofit's finances, programming, operations, and impact. Develop a fact sheet (talking points document) that highlights recent accomplishments, notable facts, and current objectives.

5. Talk less, listen more, and ask interesting questions

Major donors loathe "talkers." If you babble too much about anything, especially yourself, donors will tune you out, and close their checkbooks.

To be a good conversationalist, you need to create dialogue by getting people talking about what *they* like to talk about. Be inquisitive. Pull conversation along with good questions, timely discussions, and attentive listening. Ask donors about their background, hobbies, and philanthropic interests. Challenge yourself to listen twice as much as you talk.

6. Express your passion

Donors are curious about your relationship with your nonprofit. They want to know why you're so passionate about the nonprofit you serve. Testimonials are powerful tools of influence and persuasion, and you'll want to use them to ignite excitement in the hearts of donors.

To do this, build a few stories that explain how you got involved, why you're passionate about the mission, what you admire about your non-profit, and why you support it. Keep stories brief and practice them so you can share them with ease, confidence, and enthusiasm.

7. Live an inspired life and develop your own interests

Many donors are smart and interesting, and they like meeting smart and interesting people. The more you experience, the more knowledge you'll have to share and the more interesting you'll become. To expand your world, spend more time reading. See a play. Try new restaurants. Adopt new technology. Travel to new places. Make a point to do something new once a month. Chase your passions. Live inspired.

"Talk less. Listen more.
If you babble too much about anything,
especially yourself, donors will tune you out,
and close their checkbooks."

CHAPTER 12

INITIAL CONTACT: PREPARATION TACTICS

You have a list of donors. You know they have an interest in your mission. You've been assigned to call them, set a meeting, and make an appeal. Rainmakers know successful donor interaction starts with good preparation. Here are eight tactics you should always employ before talking or meeting with a donor.

1. Do your homework

2. Practice your pitch

3. Be a philanthropic concierge

4. If you team up, choose roles

5. Confirm the meeting

6. Invite the spouse (partner)

7. Have someone credible make an introduction

8. Bring a notepad

1. Do your homework

If you want to see how fast a donor can turn off their giving spigot, show up to a meeting unprepared. Some people can wing it, but most can't. If you flop, you will make a bad impression and possibly lose a donation—and a donor.

Read and study. What do you know about the donor? What interesting facts can you share about the issue your nonprofit is addressing? What are their philanthropic interests? Can you comfortably talk about your programs and the impact each is making? Have you reviewed your key marketing material? Do the hard work before you call or meet with a donor and your time together will be more effective.

2. Practice your pitch

Perhaps the single most important thing you can do before making contact with a donor is practicing what you want to say. Before you call, rehearse the call. Before you ask for money, rehearse the type of ask you plan to make and tactics you'll need to execute it. Rehearse the type of objections you may encounter and how you'll handle each. Create problem scenarios and then rehearse successful outcomes.

Role-playing with family, friends, and colleagues is also an effective tactic to practice and improve your techniques. Throughout the process, you will stumble and make mistakes. And yes, it can be embarrassing. However, practice builds confidence and improves technique. If you're willing to do what so many others are unwilling to do, you'll reap big rewards.

3. Be a philanthropic concierge
In their quest to make a difference, most donors, especially major donors, want to make wise social investments. Your job is to advise them why your nonprofit is a great investment and deserves support.

Before you even contact a donor, think about your personal brand. Do you want to come off as the pushy sales type? How about a desperate beggar with a tin cup? Neither, right? Rainmakers portray themselves as passionate, social investment advisors. Think "philanthropic concierge."

The concierge persona is a good one because raising money is not about sales, coercion, guilt, or convincing. It's about inspiring donors to joyfully give by educating them and creating memorable and "unexpectedly pleasurable" experiences that allow them to convince themselves that your nonprofit is a wise social investment.

To do this, you'll want to ask donors about *their* needs, desires, and interests. Ask donors why they have an interest in the issues you're addressing. What areas of your organization do they want to support? The more you help a donor realize your nonprofit is the best nonprofit to help them make a difference and achieve their philanthropic goals, the more willing they will be to say "Yes" to your appeals.

4. If you team up, choose roles
If two or more of your team members will be meeting with a donor, decide who will be responsible for talking about what topics. For example, let's say your chief executive, board chair, and a high-profile donor will be meeting a major donor for lunch.

You could designate the chief executive as the person who will facilitate the meeting and answer specific questions about your nonprofit. The donor could provide a personal story of why they're involved and offer a personal endorsement of why they think your nonprofit is worthy of support. The board chair could be assigned to make the ask. If you're organized, prepared, and have a unified message, donors will feel comfortable and you'll win the gift.

5. Confirm the meeting

Many donors are busy. They travel, run businesses, and their schedules change constantly. Things get lost in the shuffle and they forget. So whether it's your first or tenth meeting, always confirm it.

Send a brief reminder a month before the meeting and another one two weeks before the meeting. Then, two days before you meet, confirm the day, time, and place of the meeting and ask the donor if they need any support collateral other than what you've provided. Sending a simple reminder like the one below shows donors you're responsible and keep on top of priorities.

Keep the email short, no more than a handful of lines. Include pertinent information about the meeting in the subject line. Remember to include your mobile phone number and ask for theirs if you don't have it.

Subject line:
Reminder . . . Meeting with Jamie, Tue 4 p.m., Starbucks

Text:
Hi, Jim!
Looking forward to seeing you tomorrow at 4 p.m. at Starbucks.
If you hit a snag on the way, call my mobile: (xxx) xxx-xxxx.
What is your mobile number in case I need to call you last minute?
Respectfully,
Jamie~

6. Invite the spouse (partner)

If a donor has a partner, it's likely they make philanthropic decisions together. Try to get the partner involved in the process as early as possible. Invite them to join calls, cultivation events, and meetings. The partner has friends too, so if you can get him or her involved, you increase your chances of referrals, advocacy, involvement, and other unforeseen donor benefits.

7. Have someone credible make an introduction

There are many times when a board member or volunteer is the person who has the relationship with the donor but is not the person who will be meeting the donor to make an appeal. In this case, the person with the relationship should attend the first meeting, if only to introduce the prospect to the asker and establish a comfortable, friendly setting for the meeting. This tactic is called "drafting a person's reputation."

This type of introduction is also a way to establish the asker's credibility. This can be done in an email, or on a phone call, but the best introductions are made in person. For example, let's say Kim Stevens is the chief executive at ACME nonprofit. She is meeting Jessie (a potential donor) for lunch. The board chair, Jim, happens to know Jessie very well and offers to call Jessie to "warm up" the meeting between Kim and Jessie.

> "Hi, Jessie! Jim, here. It was good to see you last Friday at the gala. I understand Kim Stevens, our chief executive, is going to meet with you this Thursday for lunch. I've been giving $5,000 a year for the past five years to ACME. I believe it's the most effective hunger relief program in the city and their leadership is top notch. Kim is a star as you'll immediately see. She's also a world-class singer. Ask her about the time she sang on Broadway before moving to Kansas. It's a great story. Anyway, thanks again for meeting with her. I'm sure we'll bump into you and Jen at the gallery walk this Tuesday. Take care."

8. Bring a notepad

There can be a lot of important things to remember during an hour-long meeting with a donor so bring a notepad to take notes. Electronic tablets are okay, but use good judgment; they can be bulky and distracting, especially over lunch at a nice restaurant.

When taking notes, use shorthand. Jot down key words instead of writing full sentences so you can maintain eye contact and remain engaged in conversation. Once you leave the donor, you can write out full-length sentences from your notes when updating the donor's profile in your donor database system.

CHAPTER 13

THE DONOR LIFECYCLE

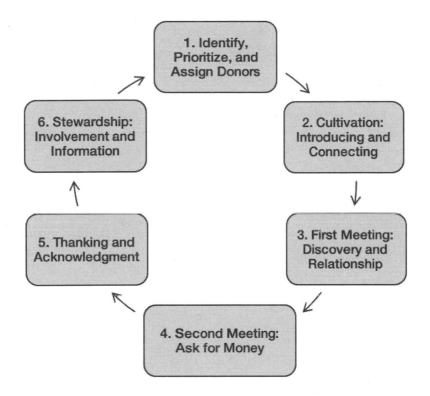

CHAPTER 14

IDENTIFYING AND FINDING DONORS

Rainmakers know donors don't stick around forever. Their interests change, they move, and they die. So whether you have five donors or 5,000, you need to make a commitment and establish a process to continually find new donors.

Doing so will not only help you raise more money, it will prevent you from losing income through donor attrition. Plus, more donors mean more income diversity, which can reduce income risk if you're overly reliant on a few major donors or large grants. What follows are some effective tactics Rainmakers use to find new donors.

Who are we looking for?

It's smart to acquire all types of donors, but Rainmakers make a special effort to work on expanding their lists of major donors. Whether you define a major donor as a person who gives $5,000 or $20,000, it doesn't matter; gifts from major donors are an efficient source of funding. Remember, it takes 200 gifts of $100 to equal one gift of $20,000.

When considering people as potential donors, no matter what their giving capacity, it's best to target people who have strong feelings about the issues you're addressing, the mission you're executing, and the people or thing you're impacting.

Next, you'll want to target people who *do not* have strong feelings about supporting issues and missions like yours, especially major donors, because they may become donors and passionate advocates of your mission after learning more about the amazing work you're doing.

For example, let's say one of your board members has an affluent widow visiting her from out of town and invites her to a cultivation event. At the event, she may learn about the urgent need to feed the hundreds of hungry children in your community and then feel compelled to learn more, get involved, and fund your work.

Build a list—start from the inside and work out

To expand your network of donors, ask people who are strongly connected with your nonprofit to provide names of potential donors. Start with your board, staff, and volunteers. Who do they know—family, friends, and business associates? How about contacts at foundations, businesses, and corporations? Always be asking for names at board meetings, staff meetings, and volunteer training sessions. More major donors mean more funding.

Who do your donors know?

Current donors can be a great source for donor referrals. They know the "who's who" in the community, trustees of large family foundations, and CEOs of major corporations. Major donors are often reluctant to give up names of their wealthy friends and contacts, but if you ask for just one or two names a year, you might find them more receptive.

Also, as donors become involved in the work of your nonprofit, you'll find they *want* to provide referrals. If they found a good investment in you, they are often eager to share their smart choice with friends. Comb your donor list. Make some calls. Go out to lunch. Ask for a referral.

Don't overlook Grandma Gini

One of the best places to find major donors is to examine your list of minor donors. Many major donors test the waters of a nonprofit with small gifts. Is there a sleeping giant in your list of minor donors? And don't forget about Grandma Gini who's been giving you $100 a year for 10 years. Rainmakers know she just might have stocks and bonds totaling millions. This is why you must value every gift and every donor. Yes, it's important to focus the majority of your time stewarding major donors, but not at the cost of neglecting minor donors.

Former residents and vacationers

Host a brainstorming session with staff and board members to come up with names of people or families that *used* to live in your area. Maybe an investment banker on Wall Street grew up hungry in your town. He may want to support your hunger relief program for kids because he doesn't want kids to suffer like he did.

Other ideas to consider: wealthy people who moved out of town, high school alumni who went on to become celebrities, and seasonal residents that want to support the communities they spend time visiting.

Collect names at special events

Many people attending fundraising and cultivation events are guests of donors. This creates a good opportunity to collect a few new names. No matter what size or type of special event you're hosting, *always* have a check-in table. It's best to have volunteers asking guests for their contact information, rather than having guests write their information. Not only is it classier, it ensures clarity and accuracy.

Collect names at public speaking opportunities

Prominent and affluent people belong to social clubs and attend events hosted by community service organizations. These organizations are always looking for guest speakers. Speaking at events like this is a favorite among Rainmakers because it's one of the most underutilized tactics for creating awareness and finding new volunteers and donors.

When speaking at an event, make sure you collect contact information. Pass out simple 4x6 cards that ask for basic contact information. Do not ask for money unless the speaking event is a fundraising event. Create plenty of space to write. Create "call-to-action" check boxes for ways they can get involved.

<u>**Example**</u>

    ❑ Yes, I would like to volunteer at the soup kitchen one night.

    ❑ Yes, I would like to help collect food from Rotary members.

    ❑ Yes, I would like to take a private tour of your warehouse.

Suggested places to speak: Elks Club, Lions Club, Kiwanis, Rotary, Chamber of Commerce, local radio or cable show, professional or business associations, networking clubs, investment clubs, college clubs, golf clubs, wine clubs, cultural events, community foundations, churches, and corporate "brown bag" lunch talks.

Get noticed

Another way to create awareness and find donors is to attend events that normally wouldn't be showcasing nonprofits. Set up a pop-up tent at a local concert, art fair, gallery walk, car show, or sporting event. Many of these events have a main stage. If they do, ask if you can make a few 30-second plugs about your nonprofit and the work you're doing, and then ask people to stop by your tent to learn more.

If you do get a chance to speak, you can use a texting service and have people in the audience text you their contact information and then follow up later. Having a free raffle item or a giveaway of some type will encourage people to stop by your tent. When they do, talk about what you do and collect their contact information.

Do reconnaissance

Collect impact reports (annual reports) from major nonprofits and scan the donor listing for potential major donors. Get on their mailing lists and subscribe to their e-newsletters. Start with local universities, private high schools, and hospitals. Next, check out impact reports from large local nonprofits (and competitors) like your neighborhood YMCA.

Then you'll want to receive impact reports from large state and national nonprofits that address the same issues as you, or serve the same sector, or serve the same types of beneficiaries. Have your board, staff, and perhaps a handful of your donors review the donor lists of these organizations and identify any donors they know or suggest contacting.

Are screening and lead services worth it?

Screening services are businesses that provide names of, and information on, donors. Fees can be hefty. For a small nonprofit, in a small community, these services are not usually worth the money unless the mission has a national or international footprint.

Why? Most affluent donors and major corporations are often reluctant to make sizable donations to small nonprofits outside their geographic region. Foundations, on the other hand, are more inclined to make these types of donations.

However, if you operate a large nonprofit based in a large city, and you're making widespread impact, either locally, nationally, or internationally, then it might be worth calling a screening service. If you do choose to use one, err on the side of caution and buy a small number of names as a trial to test the quality of the list. In some cases, the contact information will be old and inaccurate, yielding very low response rates.

"To find more donors,
do more public speaking events around town."

CHAPTER 15

PRIORITIZING AND ASSIGNING DONORS

Once you have a list of donors, current or potential, you'll need a system to prioritize (segment) and assign them. You can prioritize donors based on ability to give, probability of giving, time since last gift, size of last gift, lifetime giving, recent event attendance, passion for the mission, interest in a program, track record of supporting similar causes, or some combination of all these.

All donors are important and it's essential that you manage every donor at every giving level throughout the year. However, if you're like most nonprofits, 70 to 90 percent of the donations you receive will come from just 10 to 30 percent of your donor base.

Rainmakers know this, which is why they prioritize their lists and focus up to 50 percent of their fundraising efforts on their largest donors, or donors with the potential to make substantial gifts. If you want to make it rain big money, you'd be wise to do the same.

Assign a gift range
After prioritizing your donors, go back through the list and assign a "gift range" to each donor. Do John and Wendy Holt have the *potential* to give a gift in the $5,000-$10,000 range, or should it be $10,000-$20,000?

To determine a gift range for a donor, use past giving records, gifts made to other nonprofits, or recommendations from board members. Assigning gift ranges can be difficult because you never really know what a donor will give until you spend time with them to understand their philanthropic interests and financial position. Nonetheless, it's good to set targets and estimate the amount of funds you hope to raise.

Assign donors to team members
If the goal is to raise money from your top donors, you'll want to start by assigning team members to donors so they can set up face-to-face meetings to ask for money. This will require a set of "askers" (Chapter 4), but it may also require other team members who can support the donor management process.

For example, one asker could perform all the tasks below, but you may find it more effective to use a combination of team members based on their skills, interests, and relationships with donors.

1. **Who will make contact?**
   Determine the best person to make contact with the donor to set up an initial call, meeting, or invitation to a cultivation event. Does any team member know the donor? Does any team member know someone who knows the donor? Does any team member share a common interest, hobby, or background with the donor?

2. **Who will ask for money?**
   Determine who should ask the donor for money. It may be the same person as the contact person, or it may be one of the askers on your team. Whoever it is, the person should be experienced. The larger the donor, the more important it is to have your best Rainmakers doing the ask. You can't afford to lose a major gift due to a flubbed ask.

3. **Who will manage the relationship?**
   Determine who should manage the ongoing relationship with the donor (stewardship). This is typically the person who solicited the donor. Whoever is assigned the task should have plenty of time to make calls, write letters, and meet with the donor.

   The task of stewarding donors is arguably the most important stage of the fundraising process. A donor may give once due to a well-crafted ask, but a donor continues to give based largely on how well they were treated *after* they donated.

How many donors should you assign to each asker?
This is a difficult number to gauge. First, it depends on how many askers you have on your team. More askers mean more capacity. Second, it depends on the experience of each asker. Experienced fundraisers can handle more donors because they are more efficient. Plus, you want your inexperienced askers managing smaller donors until they become proficient to reduce the chances of flubbing an ask or offending a donor.

Third, it depends on how much time each team member can contribute. As a general guide, budget 10-20 hours a year to manage a major donor. This includes time spent on meetings, cultivation events, updating database profiles, phone calls, and back office support. Smaller donors and low-maintenance donors may only require 5-10 hours.

This means a full-time gifts officer, whose sole responsibility is managing donors, might be able to manage 120 to 180 major donors. Whereas, a chief executive who can spend only 40 percent of his time managing donors, may only be able to manage 40 to 50 major donors.

As for volunteer team members (board members), you'll be lucky if you can get one or two members willing to contribute 60 hours a year (5 hours a month) to managing donors. This is enough time to effectively manage a few major donors and a few minor donors through all stages of the donor lifecycle.

The following exercise will help you start the process of assigning donors. Once you start tracking how much time your team requires to manage its donors, you can make adjustments to accommodate the team's capacity.

Exercise

Assume it will take an average of 15 hours a year to manage major donors and 7.5 hours for small and low-maintenance donors. You will want to modify these figures after you track actual times.

1. To determine how many major donors your nonprofit can effectively manage, simply calculate how many hours each team member is willing to contribute to the task and then divide this number by 15 (or whatever number you choose) to determine how many donors the team can manage.

2. To determine how many small and low-maintenance donors your nonprofit can effectively manage, determine how many hours each member is willing to contribute to the task and then divide this number by 7.5 (or whatever number you choose) to determine how many donors the team can manage.

As you're beginning to see, high-performance fundraising is resource intensive. One person cannot do it alone—not effectively, anyway. You wouldn't expect to run a program that serves 2,000 beneficiaries with one staff member and a few volunteers, would you? Why would you expect to run a fundraising program that has 2,000 donors with one staff member and a few volunteers?

If you want your fundraising efforts to be as efficient and effective as your programming efforts, you must invest a similar level of enthusiasm, commitment, and resources.

"Rainmakers spend up to
50 percent of their fundraising efforts
on their largest donors."

CHAPTER 16

CULTIVATING DONORS

In simple terms, cultivation is the process of nurturing relationships with new donors *before* asking them for money, and stewardship is the process of nurturing relationships with existing donors *after* they make a donation. Chapter 30 covers stewardship in detail.

The general purpose of the cultivation process is to introduce new donors to your nonprofit, educate them about the issues you're addressing, expose them to the work you're doing and the people involved, and start a relationship. Rainmakers know that cultivating donors means much more than cultivating people for money, it means cultivating resources, influence, expertise, networks, and advocacy.

Types of cultivation events
There are dozens of types of cultivation events. Most events, such as facility tours, meet-and-greets, and volunteer days strictly target potential donors and there is no appeal for money involved. Other events such as wine tastings, auctions, and galas target potential donors and current donors, and include an appeal for money.

In the big scheme of fundraising, Rainmakers know cultivation is a process, not an event. Sure, a donor may make a donation at the first event they attend (if there is an ask), but in all likelihood it may take a blend of calls, emails, meetings, events, and program observations before a donor makes their first gift. In some cases, a donor may require two years of cultivation before they make a gift.

There is no perfect cultivation process. It will be different for each donor. But no matter what methods you choose to cultivate donors, and no matter how long it takes to secure a first gift, your job is to continually deepen your relationships with donors, inform them, engage them, and emotionally charge them about the work you're doing.

Ideas for Cultivation Events

1. **Give a tour.** Host an open house or give a tour of your offices or facilities. Introduce donors to staff, volunteers, board members, and beneficiaries.

50

2. **Host a small event.** Plan a small, intimate cocktail party, wine tasting, luncheon, or dinner party hosted by a board member or major donor. If appropriate, invite a few of your beneficiaries to attend the event.

3. **Host a public event.** Host a large, public event such as a concert, fun run, or gala. The larger the venue, the more important it is to spend time with donors to make them feel welcome. Assign hosts and have them introduce donors to board members and attendees.

4. **Show them what you do.** Host an event where your programming is taking place. Introduce donors to staff, volunteers, and beneficiaries. Graduation nights, award ceremonies, ribbon-cutting events, and beneficiary performances can be powerful events.

5. **Meet at a café or restaurant.** Nothing extravagant. Simple, classy, affordable, and free from distractions. Host a small breakfast or lunch gathering, or meet a donor at a nice lounge for a cocktail.

6. **Meet one-on-one.** Choose a favorite location of a donor. This could be their home, office, yacht, country club, or social club. Or, meet in an environment where they can enjoy one of their favorite recreational activities such as hiking a trail, a walk in a park, or a stroll along a beach. You may even ask a donor to join you for an athletic activity you both enjoy doing such as skiing, golfing, tennis, or attending a sporting event.

Questions for relationship building

The essence of cultivation is relationship building. Rainmakers know that the best way to get to know someone is to ask questions. The following page has a set of questions you can use to build relationships with donors.

If you're hosting a cultivation dinner party for 20, you can make a fun and classy game out of the process. On quality card stock, write out questions like the ones below. Provide some variety by choosing questions from different categories.

Pass out the cards during dinner to encourage people to get to know each other. Have people share their responses with others sitting at their table. If everyone is sitting at one or two large tables, break up the tables into groups of four or six.

Questions for Relationship Building

1. **Hobbies and interests.** What are your favorite hobbies and interests? How do you like to spend your free time? Tell me a quirky talent or hobby you have that few people know about.

2. **Family.** What does your partner enjoy doing? How did you meet? Do you have children? Tell me about them.

3. **Travel.** Tell me about the most unusual place you've traveled. Tell me about the most adventurous trip you've ever taken. Where do you plan to travel next? Why there?

4. **Business.** What business are you in? What do you do for work? How did you get started in that business or area of work? What events led up to starting your business? Why did you choose that industry? What are your business plans for the future?

5. **Community involvement.** Are you a member of any associations or clubs? Why did you join? Do you volunteer for any nonprofits or sit on the board of any nonprofits? Which ones? What inspired you to support them?

6. **Values and aspirations.** What drives you? What motivates you? What experience or event has had the greatest effect on your life? Tell me about one person who played an important role in your life. What event has brought you the most joy in life? What's one dream you're still hoping to fulfill? What social issues are you passionate about?

7. **Background.** Where's your hometown? What's it like there? How did you end up in this area? What is one of your favorite childhood memories? What was your "15 minutes of fame" experience?

8. **Sports.** What sports or leisure activities do you enjoy? Why those? Do you compete in any sport? What sports teams do you follow with passion?

9. **Education.** Where did you attend college? What did you study? What is one of your favorite college memories?

10. **Entertainment.** What is your all-time favorite band, TV show, or movie? Why that one? What were your favorite TV shows growing up? Why? What TV show do you like to watch to relax?

Questions to Understand Philanthropic Interest

It's important to get to know a donor personally, but Rainmakers also know that it's important to understand a donor's philanthropic interests, motivations, and their connection to your nonprofit. The following questions will help you probe the hearts and minds of donors, and stimulate dialogue surrounding the things that inspire them to get involved and write checks.

1. **Discovery.** How did you first learn about us? Why did you decide to volunteer? I heard you volunteered a few weeks ago; tell me about your experience. What did you think about last week's gala? How did it move you? How did your tour of our soup kitchen and food pantry touch your heart?

2. **Issues and interests.** What issues are you most passionate about? (e.g., hunger, spousal abuse, animals, seniors, the environment, etc.). What are your philanthropic interests right now? How would you like to make a difference in the world?

3. **Information.** What would you like to know about us? Have you read our impact statement? Would you like to know how we allocate funds? What would you like to know about our board, staff, volunteers, or business partners? What would you like to know about our programs or services? What problems would you like to help us solve?

4. **Opinions.** What do you think of our nonprofit? Our brand? What are our strengths? Weaknesses? If you had a magic wand, what would you like to see happen with our nonprofit?

5. **History.** What types of nonprofits have you funded? Why did you support them? Tell me about one of the best giving experiences you've ever had. What did the organization do that you liked? What did they do that made you feel good? What is the worst nonprofit investment you've ever made? Tell me about it.

6. **Performance.** When comparing equally good nonprofits, what are the top three factors you look at to help you choose one over the other? What is your expectation of how a nonprofit should treat its donors?

7. **Involvement.** How could you see yourself becoming more involved with us? If you could get more involved in just one of our programs or services, which would it be? If you were to contribute a skill, area of expertise, or connection in the community, what would it be?

Preparing for a Cultivation Event

The essence of hosting cultivation events is to educate donors about the work you're doing and inspire them to take action. If your team is unprepared to engage donors and answer their questions, your event will be a dud.

Below are a handful of tactics your team can use to prepare for a cultivation event. Have one or two meetings prior to the event to develop and assemble this information and then practice it in role-playing scenarios.

1. **Memorize.** Memorize your 30-second organizational overview (Chapter 34).

2. **Stories.** Be able to tell three stories:
   a. How you became involved, the contributions you make, what you enjoy, and why you believe in the organization.
   b. An experience you or a beneficiary had that shows the impact of the work your organization does.
   c. Why someone should support your organization.

3. **Financials.** Know these two facts about your financials:
   a. How much money goes to programs, administration, and fundraising (in percentage terms).
   b. Your current annual budget—projected income and expenses.

4. **Facts.** Study your fact sheet (Chapter 34). Know three accomplishments your organization recently achieved and three things it's doing to impact the people you serve (or the issue you're addressing) and your community.

5. **Talk.** Talk with five people during the event with the objective of getting them to say "Yes" to an invitation to observe a programming event or tour your facilities.

Planning and Hosting Cultivation Events

The larger the cultivation event, the more logistics and resources it will require. It would take an entire book to cover the details of planning and hosting every type of cultivation event because each event has specific requirements based on its intended purpose, theme, and outcome.

That said, here are five goals every event should attempt to achieve. Chapter 31 provides additional tactics on hosting events.

1. **Make an unforgettable first impression.** Rainmakers know that first impressions are lasting impressions. Develop specific and creative strategies on how your team will welcome donors the minute they walk through the doors of your event. Also, collect contact information if you don't already have it.

2. **Get people to mingle.** Develop creative ways for people to meet each other before the event gets underway. Have event ambassadors introduce themselves to donors and make introductions to other attendees. Have "get to know you" questions written on cards that donors answer with others sitting at their table.

3. **Involve your beneficiaries.** Whenever possible and appropriate, integrate beneficiaries into the event (pre-event coaching is a must). Have them sit among donors so they can share their stories and answer questions, or have one or two speak to the entire group. Integrating key staff and volunteers can also be an effective tactic.

4. **Never bore people.** All videos, speeches, and skits should be *brief,* compelling, powerful, and memorable. Use your best speakers. Your guests should leave an event feeling moved, inspired, and motivated.

5. **Tell people how you plan to follow up.** You invited donors to your event for a reason so don't leave them wondering what's supposed to happen next. "We're grateful you attended tonight's event. Your table ambassador will call you next week to set up a time to tour our warehouse and see our new soup kitchen in action."

Cultivation events – who does the work?
Everyone. Do not throw the work of cultivation events on the backs of staff. All events require time, effort, and resources, and some require

hundreds of hours of work. Cultivation events provide good opportunities for board members who say, "I'm not good at asking for money," to volunteer some time, expertise, and influence to support the fundraising efforts of their nonprofits.

Working together not only leads to well-organized events, it builds team culture between board members, staff, and volunteers, uniting them around a common purpose everyone cares so much about.

Patience with the process

A surefire way to lose a new donor is to pressure them. The road to successful cultivation is patience and gentle perseverance. Cultivation is a little like dating; if you want to win the admiration of donors, you'll need to go slowly, be respectful, show humility, and use good manners. If you rush the process, donors will push away and avoid your calls.

How long should you cultivate donors if they aren't responding? Until they say stop. Many donors are busy. Rainmakers know that if a donor turns down one or two event invitations, it doesn't mean they're not interested in supporting your mission, though it could because some donors want to stop giving but lack the courage to say so. Rather, it may just mean, "I have too much going on right now," or "The timing is bad."

Be respectful and patient, and continue cultivating a donor until they tell you in one form or another, "I'm not interested in supporting you so please remove me from your list and stop contacting me." Until you hear words to this effect, keep trying.

"The road to successful cultivation is patience and gentle perseverance."

CHAPTER 17

INITIAL CALL:
SETTING UP THE FIRST MEETING

Rainmakers spend a lot of time setting up meetings with donors in face-to-face settings because they know it's one of the most effective ways to raise money. An old maxim in fundraising is not only wise advice, it's an imperative: "No meeting, no money!"

As you recall, if a donor knows you and has an emotional connection to the work of your nonprofit, there is a 70 percent chance they'll make a donation if you ask in a face-to-face setting. If they are also engaged in the work of your mission by volunteering in some capacity, the odds of them saying "Yes" to your ask can top 90 percent.

These are amazing odds and should provide all the incentive you need to set up as many meetings as possible.

Face-to-face settings include one-on-one meetings, dinner parties, fundraising events, and galas where you make in-person appeals. Most of the face-to-face references in this book refer to one-on-one meetings and small, specialty events because they are typically the most effective places to raise money from your largest donors who are responsible for 70 to 90 percent of the income you raise from individuals.

Use the following tactics to land your first meeting with a donor, or a primary contact at a corporation or family foundation.

How to Land Your First Meeting

1. Keep your eye on the prize
As a Rainmaker, your objective is to set up a series of meetings with your top donors to build relationships and raise money. The purpose of the first meeting is for you to get to know a donor and for them to get to know you and your nonprofit (more about this later). But to get a first meeting, you must start by making a phone call.

2. Use the phone!

Never text or email a donor to set up a first-time meeting unless specifically requested by a donor to do so. Pick up the phone, call a donor, and ask them to join you for coffee, breakfast, lunch, a hike, or a meeting at their office or yours.

3. Keep it short

When you call a donor, keep it short. If you respect a donor's time, they will reward you. In general, keep the call to three minutes or less, unless the donor starts asking questions and carrying the conversation. Even then, keep the call brief. Your goal is to be friendly, professional, and set a meeting. You'll have plenty of time to talk when you meet.

4. Be positive and confident

Speak in a tone that expresses your enthusiasm and confidence for the mission and your relationship with the donor. Waves of positive energy should resonate from your voice and body language.

5. Prepare and practice three scripts

Having scripts and practicing them are two major differentiators between a Rainmaker and the average fundraiser. Develop at least three scripts and practice the one you plan to use on the call. After the call, modify the script based on what you learned during the call. You'll find examples of phone scripts in upcoming chapters.

6. Make friends with the gatekeeper

When you make a call, you may not get to talk with the donor. A "gatekeeper" may be screening their calls. This person could be a personal assistant, foundation trustee, or son-in-law.

Rainmakers know it's smart business to make friends with gatekeepers. They often have inside information, strong ties to donors, and authority to make key decisions. In fact, you may be talking with the donor's gatekeeper more than you talk with them.

That's fine. If a gatekeeper likes you, you're in; if you're rude and disrespectful, you're doomed. Always treat them with respect and dignity. Be gracious and grateful, and say "thank you" a lot.

If you're having difficulty getting a meeting with a donor, ask the gatekeeper their opinion on how you should proceed:

"When is Mrs. Smith returning?"

"May I make an appointment with Mrs. Smith through you?"

"Is there a time of day Mrs. Smith prefers to have meetings?"

"What would you suggest I do to follow up?"

"What is the best way to set up a meeting with Mrs. Smith?"

7. Be kind, patient, and persistent

Setting up a meeting with a donor can be a time of frustration. Many donors lead busy lives. They own businesses, travel, maintain hectic social schedules, and get bombarded with funding requests from nonprofits. You may ask kindly for a meeting and still not get one.

However, failing to get a meeting does not mean a donor isn't interested in supporting you; it may just mean the timing isn't right. Respecting their time and personal space, as well as their gatekeeper's time and space, will go a long way toward establishing the relationship and credibility you desire—and getting a meeting.

If you are kind, grateful, patient, and persistent, you'll get your meeting. Don't give up calling until you get a flat out "No" of some sort.

8. Leave a voice message

If you call and get a donor's voicemail, leave a message. Hanging up is rude. When you leave a message, keep it short and specific. Long messages are irritating. State your name, organization, association with the organization, and be sure to leave your phone number toward the *beginning* of your message.

Be kind and polite. Speak slowly and clearly, especially when leaving your phone number, which you should say twice. Keep the message simple. Ask the donor to call you back and if you don't hear back by a certain time, you'll call back. Until you're comfortable, you may want to write out scripts for your messages.

"Hi, Mr. Jones! This is Tom Iselin, founder of The Hunger Coalition. Please call me at your convenience. You can reach me at xxx.xxx.xxxx. If I don't hear back by Friday, I'll call back early next week. Again, it's Tom Iselin calling from The Hunger Coalition at xxx.xxx.xxxx. Have a great day . . . goodbye!"

9. Avoid making appeals during a phone call

Making a phone appeal to a smaller donor is fine. However, try to avoid accepting a gift from a first-time major donor over the phone. The donor may insist, or ask you to "send some information in the mail," but this is giving them an easy way out. When this happens—and it will—*tactfully* flank the response and continue to try to set up a meeting.

Remember, one of your key objectives, which arguably is more important than getting a donation, is making a personal connection with a donor and building a relationship, neither of which can be done very well on the phone. To do this, you need to get the donor to commit to an in-person meeting and get off the phone.

In the end, if the donor is adamant about making a gift on the phone, or if they want you to send an appeal letter in the mail, then grant the wishes of the donor; perhaps you can meet them another time. But don't acquiesce early on; do your best to secure a meeting.

"Sorry, Tom, I'm very busy and do not have time to meet. Just send me a donor packet or a pledge card and I'll make a donation."

"What a nice offer, John. Thank you! However, I want to get to know you because The Hunger Coalition cares about its donors more than their donations. We treat our donors with respect. We want to inform you, involve you, listen to you, and help you achieve your philanthropic goals. That's why it's important for us to build a relationship with you, John, and we both know that the only way to do this well is to spend time together. Plus, I guarantee your appreciation of our programs will deepen once you see the kids in action. You can carve out an hour to see our kids in action, can't you?"

"Sure. But I'm out of town for the next two weeks."

"I understand. May I book a time with your assistant for the first week of June?"

"That should work."

"Great, I'll send a reminder email a few days before the meeting along with directions. Have a great day . . ."

"Take this to heart:
No meeting, no money!"

CHAPTER 18

INITIAL CALL:
5-STEP SCRIPT FORMULA

You just read a script on how to make a call to set up a first-time meeting with a donor. That's one example. As a Rainmaker, you'll want to write a number of scripts. To help you do that, use the script formula below; it provides the basic elements you need to write winning scripts to secure meetings.

As your confidence builds, you'll be able to rely less on scripts and more on your experience as the basic elements of the script formula become a natural way of talking with donors.

Initial Call: 5-Step Script Formula

1. Identify yourself

2. Start with pleasantries

3. State your intention

4. Provide mosquito repellent

5. Ask for a date

1. Identify yourself
This seems obvious, but many people wait too long to identify themselves, or they don't provide enough information. Donors are busy. They receive a lot of calls from friends, business associates, and hucksters. To put a donor at ease, state your name, title, and the name of your nonprofit.

"Hi, Emily, this is Tom Iselin, founder of The Hunger Coalition . . ."

2. Start with pleasantries
Strong relationship. If the strength of your relationship with a donor is good to strong, make some small talk to break the ice, but keep it brief—one to three minutes. Topics? How about the donor's hobbies, work, family, connection to your nonprofit, connection to you, or current events?

> "How are the kids? I heard the high school football team won a close game on Friday. Did Jeremy start as running back?"

No or weak relationship. If you don't know the donor, or your relationship consists of little more than a casual greeting at a party, or a shared mutual friend, the donor will be curious why you called. If the donor has supported your nonprofit in any way, or has a connection to it, start off the call by acknowledging them for it.

> "I want to thank you for taking a tour of our facilities last Friday. What was your impression of the new learning center?"

> "On behalf of the staff and board, we want to thank you for your gracious and loyal giving. Your support helped more than 1,000 veterans secure jobs last year."

If you don't know the donor and the donor has no connection to your nonprofit, you can still use an icebreaker of some type, but make it quick and keep it generic. Comment on the weather, a local piece of news, or make a personal gesture. Since the donor will be curious about why you're calling, it's more important to state your intention than to make small talk; you can always circle back to pleasantries later in the call.

> "It sure is pouring outside, isn't it? I haven't seen it rain this hard in years, have you?"

> "I know you're busy, Kari, but I promise this call will only take a few minutes. May I have a few minutes?"

3. State your intention

From the moment you identify yourself, a donor is asking, "Why is this person calling me?" By stating the intentions of your call early on, you answer this question and set expectations for the call. It also helps lower a donor's guard.

The intentions you share will vary depending on the donor and the purpose of your call. A Rainmaker's go-to intention, whether it's a first-time or longtime donor, is telling a donor you want to meet with them to talk about the work and impact of your nonprofit.

Other commonly used intentions are getting to know each other, answering questions, discussing renewal, and talking about how a donor's gift is making a difference.

> "The purpose of my call is to set up a time to meet with you to discuss the work and impact of The Hunger Coalition."

> "I'm calling to set a time to meet with you to talk about the impact your gift has made during the last year and our vision to serve more children this year."

4. Provide mosquito repellent

If you're setting up a first-time meeting with a donor, tell them you WILL NOT be asking for money during the meeting. This removes the pressure they might be feeling about giving money and the pressure you might be feeling about asking for money.

Nonetheless, when you attend the meeting, you should be prepared to work through an appeal process if the donor decides they want to make a donation.

> "And, Gary . . . I want you to know that I will not be asking for a donation of any type."

> "You have my word, I will not ask you for a dime."

> "I promise, this is strictly a time for you to get to know The Hunger Coalition better; I will not be asking you for a donation."

5. Ask for a date

When asking a donor for a date and time to meet, always provide a set of choices because people tend to answer affirmatively when given a choice. After you ask, be quiet and wait for the donor to respond before saying anything.

If the donor can meet at one of the times you suggested, thank them, tell them you'll send a reminder email, and then politely say goodbye. If the donor can't meet at the times you suggest, ask them what times would work best.

> "Would next Wednesday or Thursday work, say 10 a.m. at your office?"

> "I would enjoy showing you our new facility, would you like to meet here next Monday or Tuesday, say 1 p.m. or 2 p.m.?"

> "I'm sorry those times don't work for you. What availability do you have in the next two weeks? Mornings are typically best for me."

Example

Identify
[You] "Hi, Keith, this is Tom Iselin, founder of The Hunger Coalition."

Pleasantry
[You] "We met last week at the gala and, like I promised, I'm calling to follow up."

[Donor] "Oh, yes, I remember."

[You] "What did you think of the event?"

[Donor] "I thought the event was good, the concept of the 'empty bowl' dinner took everyone by surprise, but it was a very effective method of showing how little food the average hungry person eats for dinner."

Intention
[You] "It was a powerful moment and my wife is still talking about it. Keith, I would like to schedule a time for us to meet. My intention is to share some details about what The Hunger Coalition is doing to end child hunger in town, answer your questions, and get to know you."

Repellent
[You] "And guess what? You can rest easy because I promise not to ask you for money."

[Donor] "Funny, Tom, that's what they all say."

[You] "No, really. You have my word."

Date
[You] "I can meet you at your office next Thursday or Friday at 11 a.m. or noon. Do any of these times work?"

[Donor] "I can give you an hour next Friday at 11 a.m."

[You] "Great! I'll send you a calendar invite today and a reminder email next Wednesday, okay?"

[Donor] "Sounds good."

[You] "Great! Thank you. Have a nice day! . . . Goodbye."

[Donor] "Goodbye."

"Smile when you dial.
More than 80 percent of the message
you project over the phone is tone of voice."

CHAPTER 19

INITIAL CALL: HANDLING OBJECTIONS

Most donors lead active lives. Their time is limited and people and businesses of all types are competing to get a sliver of it. Therefore, until you build a strong relationship with a donor, you should expect that getting your sliver of time will require some tact and tenacity.

Donors come up with dozens of objections (reasons and excuses) to decline a request to meet. You could attempt to write scripts to address every conceivable objection, but Rainmakers know it's a futile task. Instead they focus on using a simple *process* like the one below that they can apply to just about any objection.

Learn the objection process below. When a donor gives you an excuse or reason for not wanting to meet, apply and repeat it until the donor says "Yes" to a meeting, clearly states they don't want to meet with you, wants to make a donation without meeting, or suggests other next steps.

3-Step Process for Handling Objections

1. *Acknowledge.* Acknowledge the objection with empathy

2. *Options.* Provide options in an effort to find a solution

3. *Close.* Close with another ask or agree to next steps

1. Acknowledge the objection with empathy
When people object to anything you're asking for, it's imperative that you immediately acknowledge (validate) their reason or excuse with empathy.

2. Provide options in an effort to find a solution
To offer options to the donor, leading to a solution, use transition words and phrases to move from your acknowledgment back to the ask.

- However, and, but, yet, so, so that, given that

- With that in mind, then again, on the other hand
- How about, even though, in fact, nevertheless
- Instead, in order, rather than, as much as, assuming that

3. Close with another ask or agree to next steps

Once you provide a new option, press on with your attempt to set up a meeting or agree to next steps.

* * * * *

Objection 1: Donor is too busy to meet with you

Acknowledge. "I understand you're busy . . .

Option. AND to accommodate your hectic schedule, I'm willing to meet you at your office for 30 minutes at a time that works for you . . .

Close. Would next Thursday at 10 a.m. at your office work?"

Objection 2: Donor feels it's unnecessary to meet

Acknowledge. "I can see how you may feel it's unnecessary to meet and I understand that you're a busy CEO . . .

Option. BUT we care about the people who support us. We don't want people to feel used. We take donor stewardship seriously. We want you to feel connected to The Hunger Coalition, not only through the work we do, but also to the people doing the work . . .

Close. What better way to do that than to meet face-to-face to learn about the organization and get to know each other. I promise to keep our first meeting to 30 minutes. So, would next Thursday at 10 a.m. at your office work?"

Objection 3: You called at a bad time

Acknowledge. "Sara, I'm sorry that I called at a bad time . . .

Option. SO here's what I can do . . .

Close. I can talk with your assistant to schedule a 30-minute meeting or I can call back at a more convenient time. Which do you prefer? . . . Ok, I'm happy to call back. What time next week works best for you? I'm available next Tuesday or Friday anytime before 10 a.m."

Objection 4: Donor already feels informed

Acknowledge. "Yes, I know you attended our fundraising gala and learned about the amazing work we're doing . . .

Option. BUT the reason I want to meet with you is SO THAT we can get to know each other and so I can answer specific questions you may have in person . . . The phone can be so impersonal and The Hunger Coalition takes pride in getting to know the people who care about the issue of child hunger here in Salem . . .

Close. If it will be more convenient for you, I can meet you and your husband at your home in the evening some night—I'll even bring a bottle of wine! Why don't you talk this over with your husband and I'll call early next week to work out a time to get together that works for both of you . . .

Repellent. And Sara, like I promised, I won't ask for money!"

Objection 5. Donor wants to make a donation on the phone

Acknowledge. "Wow . . . Dan! I'm touched that you're willing to make a donation right now . . .

Option. HOWEVER, there is so much I want to share with you about our new program and our new classrooms. It's important and exciting, and there is no way I can share it over the phone in a couple of minutes. Meeting in person will be much more personal and give us a chance to get to know each other and for you to learn the details of what we're doing to help veterans find homes . . .

Close. So, will next Tuesday or Wednesday at 11 a.m. at the Starbucks next to your office complex work for you?"

You're getting the silent treatment

Donors don't return calls for many reasons. They might be out of town, on a business trip, or on a family trip in the Caribbean. They might be testing your patience, or they just might be hoping you'll "go away" because they don't want to donate.

It's important to be persistent, but not at the risk of being annoying. It's a fine balance. If a donor is not responding after *four* phone attempts over a period of four weeks, try sending an email.

When Rainmakers get the silent treatment, they often write a humorous email like the one on the next page. Done well, a donor will respond 90 percent of the time.

Hi, Dan!

I know you're busy and probably have a good reason for not being able to return my calls.

Your time is valuable and I respect that, so please check one of the boxes and return this email.

❑ I'm parasailing in the Caribbean and haven't had a chance to respond. ☺

❑ I'm buried with work and family. Call me next week and we'll talk.

❑ I'm interested in talking with you and will call soon; please be patient.

❑ Call me back at: Time_____ Day:_____

❑ Thank you, but I have no interest in your organization.

❑ Other:

Respectfully,

Tom~

"It's important to be persistent,
but not at the risk of being annoying."

CHAPTER 20

FIRST MEETING:
DISCOVERY AND RELATIONSHIP

The first face-to-face meeting with a donor should be exploratory in nature. Your primary objective should be for you and the donor to get to know each other, learn about their philanthropic interests, and share information about the issues you're addressing, the work you're doing, and the impact your work is having. If the first meeting goes well, and you get a second meeting, your chances of getting a donation will be greater than 70 percent.

Each donor will have varying degrees of knowledge and experience of you and your nonprofit. This means you'll need to assess each donor to determine what combination of tactics you'll need to apply to effectively inform a donor, build a relationship, and ignite an emotional fire that will inspire them to say "Yes" when you make an ask.

Tactics for a successful face-to-face meeting

Rainmakers know the likelihood of a second meeting, and a chance for a donation, goes up dramatically if the first meeting goes well. Below are 10 tactics you'll want to apply to ensure your first meeting is a smooth and successful one.

Wait! What if you can't meet face-to-face with the donor? No problem. Apply as many of the following tactics as you can on a phone call, Skype call, or videoconference call.

Tactics for a Successful
Face-to-Face Meeting

1. Choose a setting that matches the donor's style

2. Be the captain of the meeting

3. Get to know them

4. Have them get to know you

5. Seek alignment as you share stories and information

6. Don't ask for money . . . but be prepared

7. Set up a second meeting

8. Stop before the end time

9. Express gratitude when saying goodbye

10. Follow up immediately after the meeting

1. Choose a setting that matches the donor's style

Rainmakers know there is no "ideal" setting for a first meeting. A lot depends on a donor's style. This means you might be holding meetings at homes, businesses, country clubs, coffee shops, ski slopes, hiking trails, and art galleries. All are good.

The best approach is to ask a donor where they would like to meet, but if they hesitate, be ready with a couple of suggestions. It's not so much about the place, but the *environment*. Choose an environment in which they will feel comfortable, and one that will allow you to talk with minimal distractions from people and noise.

If you choose to meet a donor at a restaurant or café, choose one that's pleasant and perhaps a little stylish, but not extravagant. You don't want to appear wasteful or send a message that you're trying to "impress."

However, if you want to make a lasting impression, discreetly pick up the tab. To do this, arrive at the restaurant early and give a credit card to your server. Tell him to use your card to pay the bill and add on a pre-determined tip. When you finish eating, have him bring the bill (paid). This is a classy and smooth gesture, and donors will be grateful and impressed.

2. Be the captain of the meeting

Once the meeting is underway, it's your job to control the tempo, tone, and topics of the conversation. A good rule-of-thumb is to keep the conversation genuine, personal, and two-way. If the conversation happens to veer off on a tangent, so be it. Go with the flow and when the moment is right, gently nudge the conversation back on track so you achieve your objectives.

3. Get to know them

The goal of getting to know a donor and establishing a relationship requires you to keep the focus on *them*. Start the conversation with simple pleasantries. After things warm up, glide into deeper conversation by talking about their interests, hobbies, family, interest in your mission, and philanthropic goals.

Your goal is to develop a personal and professional relationship with a donor through two-way dialogue, rather than make them feel like they're attending a sales call or undergoing a badgering interview by a talk show host. Focus on being a good listener and asking open-ended questions that encourage them to talk.

> "Sarah, how did you meet our board chair, John?" "Why did you and Bill decide to move here from your home in Basel?" "What did you enjoy most about working at the embassy in Switzerland?"

Quick tip: If the donor is not speaking at least 60 percent of the time, you're talking too much.

4. Have them get to know you

Donors like to do business with people they like and trust. If a donor doesn't ask you personal questions, inject a few snippets at a suitable moment. Be humble and sincere, but be confident about sharing your successes and background. Donors are especially interested in knowing how you got involved with your nonprofit and why you're passionate about the cause.

Keep your "bio" to two minutes or less. What's most important is letting donors *see* your excitement through your warm smile and positive body language. Let them *feel* your enthusiasm when you tell them what motivates you to work tirelessly for your cause, and let them *hear* your passion through the upbeat tone in your voice.

5. Seek alignment as you share stories and information

Building strong relationships is essential to creating loyal and generous donors. Rainmakers know the essence of donor giving is based on the simple premise that donors want to make a difference with the money they donate that's directed toward an issue they care about and a mission they believe in.

Your job? Prove to donors that you have a worthy nonprofit that can help them fulfill their philanthropic goals. The more alignment you can show, the greater your chance of a donation. To ensure that you can make a good "case for support" and show alignment, you need to be prepared to answer questions, share compelling stories, and provide convincing facts that inspire, satisfy, and motivate.

This is why it's important that you engage yourself in all types of work at your nonprofit: programming, operations, fundraising, and outreach. The more you're involved, the more stories you'll have to share—not only your own stories, but stories you've heard from beneficiaries, staff, and volunteers. If you're not involved, you'll have no personal stories to share.

Donors are emotionally inspired by powerful stories, but you also need to appeal to their rational selves by demonstrating that you run a high-performance organization. To sound credible and convincing, you need to spend time memorizing important figures from your budget, financials, strategic plan, and impact report.

Know key facts about operations, program accomplishments, and fundraising milestones. Learn the history of your nonprofit and make sure you can talk about how each of your programs and services operate, and the benefit and impact they provide. In the end, to consistently win the gifts from donors, Rainmakers know they need to touch hearts, persuade minds, and find alignment.

6. Don't ask for money . . . but be prepared

The goal of the first meeting is to establish a relationship with the donor, educate them about your nonprofit, and set up a second meeting—the ask meeting. Remember, you promised the donor that you would not ask for money during the meeting, so don't.

In fact, it's a good idea to reassure the donor of this promise by restating it after the initial pleasantries of the meeting.

> "Jessie, I want to start this discovery meeting by saying that I have no intention of asking you for money today. My purpose is to get to know you, for you to get to know me, and for you to learn more about the vital work we're doing to help veterans."

But what if the donor offers to make a donation? Then what? Well, then great! This is why you need to come to the discovery meeting prepared to handle an ask. The following chapters cover all sorts of tactics you can apply to secure a donation, no matter when or where it happens.

Always be grateful to accept a donation, but sometimes it's a smart strategy to tell the donor you'd like them to hold off on making a gift until they see your programming in action. Why? Because Rainmakers know that if they ask a donor for a gift at a location where their programming is taking place, the check size is typically much larger, sometimes as much as 50 percent larger.

Securing a gift in the moment, or delaying it in hopes of getting a larger gift later, is a judgment call. Trust your discernment and make a wise decision.

7. Set up a second meeting

The first meeting is one of discovery. You learn about the donor and they learn about you. You share stories and information, answer questions, and keep your promise of not asking for a donation. If all goes well, the donor's disposition will be upbeat and positive. Your task now is to set up a second meeting to deepen their emotional connection to your cause and the work you're doing.

You can do this by inviting a donor to observe a class where you teach autistic kids how to read. Invite them to see your modest offices where so much productivity takes place with so few resources. Invite them to meet your amazing staff and volunteers, and to interact with your beneficiaries. When they do this, their heart will be glued to your mission and their checkbook will gladly open to your funding request.

Ask for the second meeting at the first meeting. Carry your calendar. Set up the second meeting within a month of the first meeting. Two weeks or less is best. If the donor cannot commit to a date on the spot, follow up within two days to set a meeting.

> "I understand you need to check with your assistant. I'll send an email on Tuesday to see what day is best during the first week of June. Will that work?"

8. Stop before the end time

Keep the first meeting to an hour or less. About 15 minutes before the end of the meeting, ask the donor "Are we okay on time?" Read the donor's body language. End the meeting if you sense they want, or need, to go. Keeping the meeting under the allotted time will earn you a big slice of respect and credibility. Donors are busy. If they feel you are wasting their time, you will get less of their time, and money, in the future.

9. Express gratitude when saying goodbye

When Rainmakers say goodbye, they keep it simple. Summarize important points of the meeting, how you plan to follow up, and what plans you agreed on for the next meeting. Express your gratitude for the time they took to meet with you, shake hands with a warm and grateful smile, and let them know that you're looking forward to seeing them again soon.

Quick tip: If the situation presents itself, point out a segment of the meeting you enjoyed when saying goodbye. "Oh, and thank you for sharing that wild story of how you survived five days in the Alaska tundra after your plane had an emergency landing. It was fascinating! Have a great day . . . goodbye."

10. Follow up immediately after the meeting

When you get back to the office, add the notes you took during the meeting to the donor's profile in your donor database system. If you're a board member and don't have access to the system, email your notes to a staff member who can update the profile.

During the meeting, a donor may request information you did not have on hand. They may ask for a proposal they can share with trustees of their family foundation, a budget to review, or an annual report to read. If possible, respond to the donor's request within 24 hours.

If it will take more than three days to respond, email the donor on the second day and let them know when they can expect to receive the information you promised to send. Rainmakers follow up promptly because it shows donors you are responsible and reliable, and donors enjoy giving to people they can count on.

CHAPTER 21

THE ASK:
PREPARATION

The purpose of an ask meeting is straightforward: to ask for money. If you've done your job as a Rainmaker, your donors are ready. You've spent months, maybe years, cultivating first-time donors and stewarding current donors. The goal now is to meet with donors in face-to-face settings and ask for donations. It's that simple.

Well, not exactly. A lot can go wrong during an ask meeting, which is why you need to prepare. Below are eight preparation tactics you can use to ensure your meetings are fruitful and run smoothly.

The Ask Meeting: Preparation Tactics

1. Start with the right mindset
2. Include the partner early on
3. Send out a reminder
4. Location, location, location!
5. Use scripts
6. Bring your tools
7. Two heads are better than one—sometimes
8. Transport your nonprofit to the donor

1. Start with the right mindset

Before you attend any meeting with a donor, remind yourself of the fundamental reason you're meeting: to help them achieve their philanthropic goals and "make a difference" with the monetary and nonmonetary gifts they give you. The more effectively you can show them that your nonprofit is the best choice to help them accomplish these goals, the greater your chance of getting a donation and creating or retaining a loyal donor.

Also, remind yourself to never make a donor feel pressured, sold, obligated, or guilty. One of the best compliments you can receive from a donor at the time of an ask is not having to ask for a donation—they offer to make one.

> "Tom, I can't believe the incredible work you're doing with The Hunger Coalition. You have a great staff, efficient operations, sustainable funding, an engaged board, and you're working miracles. You've helped an entire segment of people in this town who were once scrounging garbage cans for meals to a state of self-sufficiency through your training and job placement programs. Amazing! I'm all in! I want to give you a check for $5,000 and start volunteering."

2. Include the partner early on
Rainmakers know most donors with partners typically make philanthropic decisions together. If your donor has a partner, always invite that person and try to get the partner involved in the donor cycle as early as possible. This way, both people will be moving through the cycle at the same time.

Otherwise, with only one partner committed, you'll often spend hours preparing for a meeting only to hear, "Well, this all sounds good, but I think we should fold my wife into the picture and hear her thoughts."

3. Send out a reminder
A day or two before the meeting, send the donor a simple reminder. A brief to-the-point email or text works best.

> *Subject line:*
> Meeting with Tom Iselin—4 p.m. at The Hunger Coalition
>
> *Body text:*
> Hi, John!
>
> Just a reminder . . . My staff is looking forward to meeting you and Jane this Wednesday, August 24, at 4 p.m. We're excited to show you our new soup kitchen in action during the dinner hour. You'll also get to see our newly refurbished food warehouse and meet some of the mothers who've gone through the program and now volunteer.
>
> There's plenty of parking around back, next to the large oak trees. Dress casually and wear comfortable shoes.
>
> Respectfully,
>
> Tom~

4. Location, location, location!

There are many useful tactics in this book to help you raise money, but few are more important than this one: The best place to ask donors for money is at a location where they can see your programs, services, or operations in action.

This tactic is extremely effective because the more donors see and interact with the work you're doing, the more emotionally connected they become to the issues you're addressing and the work you're doing, and the greater the likelihood they will make a donation. If they do make a donation, it's typically much larger than one they would have made if you had asked them at their office, home, or at a café.

This tactic is a favorite among Rainmakers because they know donors have a very difficult time saying "No" to asks when they are at a location where programming is taking place, or in the presence of staff and beneficiaries.

Quick Tip: Make a donor feel like an insider by setting up a "private" tour of your warehouse, facility, or programming that is not generally seen by others. Show them the land you're saving, the animals you're sheltering, the school you're rebuilding, the kids you're feeding, or the new YMCA you're building.

5. Use scripts

Rainmakers use scripts for a reason—they work! The purpose of a script is to help you practice the general flow of a specific type of ask. This means you'll want to design a script for the type of ask you intend to make. Use components of the 3-Step Process in the next chapter to help you write your scripts.

Once you write a script, you need to practice it—a lot! The goal is not to "memorize" a script. Rather, use it as a guideline to provide structure and flow to your ask, and to give you confidence.

This is why it's important to use your own words when writing scripts—so they sound natural. Also, create a system to archive scripts so everyone on your team can have a resource for sharing and finding examples.

6. Bring your tools

When you arrive at the meeting, you want to look and act organized. Bring a small notepad to write notes and have all your documents neatly organized into a thin folder or three-ring binder.

Here are the key items you'll want to have on hand:

1. A gift table, sponsorship infographic, or matching gift pyramid. These props can make asking easy. They provide simple, visual aids that outline donation options (Chapter 23).

2. A set of essential collateral from your marketing quiver (Chapter 34). At a minimum, include your impact report, fact sheet, program descriptions, financials, budget, and any support material you feel might appeal to the donor.

3. Copies of documents the donor requested you prepare for the meeting (e.g., appeal letter, proposal, spreadsheet, etc.). You may need to refer to these documents so make a copy for yourself.

   If a donor asks you to prepare a proposal, never send it before the meeting. Show it only *after* you've made the ask. Why? First, you don't want a donor to reject the proposal before you meet. And second, it can be a distraction during the meeting. You want to maintain eye contact and keep the donor engaged as you discuss the proposal's content.

7. Two heads are better than one—sometimes

When talking with major donors, it may be helpful to have two or three people present during the meeting. You may want the chief executive present because they can effortlessly answer any question about your nonprofit. You may want an influential board member present because they can provide stature.

You may want to include the founder, whose charisma and charm can provide credibility and appeal. You may want program staff who have been in the trenches, whose stories can provide emotional depth to the atmosphere, and you may even want a beneficiary who can provide an emotional story of how your services transformed their life.

You'll find most ask meetings only require an asker because if a donor has been properly cultivated or stewarded, they've already met board members, staff, volunteers, and beneficiaries. Therefore, if you do invite people to join your meeting, it's important that everyone provides value. Otherwise, they may become distractions.

8. Transport your nonprofit to the donor

Logistics may prevent a donor from seeing your programs and operations in action. They may live out of state. You may not have a facility, or you may have a program that operates overseas. In situations like these, you need to bring your programming, facilities, and beneficiaries to the donor.

One of the best ways to do this is to show the donor a video. If a video is powerful and compelling, it may be enough to emotionally ignite and inspire them to say "Yes" when you ask for a donation. Skype calls and videoconferencing are good tactics too. If you're doing work overseas, set up a call with a field officer and a few beneficiaries to let a donor see live footage and hear firsthand accounts of the impact your work is making.

If you plan to show a video or host a Skype call, try to do it on a TV monitor. Laptop screens and iPad screens will do the job, but a large screen with better sound will provide greater impact. Also, choose a location to show the video where distractions and disruptions will be minimal, and you can control the lighting: a donor's home, your office, a classy conference room, or a private room at a country club.

"The best place to ask donors for money is at a location where donors can see your programs, services, or operations in action."

CHAPTER 22

THE ASK:
3-STEP PROCESS

There is no perfect ask. Rainmakers know the most important thing to do to get a "Yes" to an ask is to properly cultivate and steward donors *before* asking for donations. If you've done a good job prepping a first-time donor there is a 70 percent chance you'll get a donation just by asking for one. This percentage can top 90 percent if it's a current donor who loves your mission and faithfully volunteers.

However, it would be a shame if you did the hard work to prepare a donor and then lost a gift, or received a much smaller gift, because you flubbed the ask. Rainmakers ensure their ask meetings are successful by following a three-step *process* to manage the flow of a meeting. An effective ask meeting can take as little as 15 minutes, or up to an hour. A good target is 40 minutes.

The Ask: 3-Step Process

1. The set up
1. Exchange pleasantries
2. Connect, swap stories, and talk about programs
3. Touch a heart as you make your case

2. The ask
1. The right moment
2. Ask for a specific amount of money, but be reasonable
3. State the specific use
4. Present your giving prop (visual aid) if you are using one
5. Stop talking and listen
6. Discuss the details and handle objections

3. The finishing touches
1. Thank, summarize, and discuss next steps
2. Discuss gift structure and recognition
3. Follow through

THE SET UP

1. Exchange pleasantries

Start the meeting by making introductions for any new people who might be attending. After that, engage in a few minutes of pleasantries and small talk. Thank them for meeting you. Catch up on shared interests, people you know, the weather, their family, and lighthearted news. Keep it simple and affable.

2. Connect, swap stories, and talk about programs

After small talk and pleasantries, shift the conversation to talking about your programs or services. Ask the donor two or three questions that relate to *their* involvement and interest in your programs or services. Create some dialogue around each answer, injecting support information and brief comments, when needed, and then ask another question.

The goal is to get the donor talking about their connection to your non-profit through their experiences, feelings, and thoughts. That's right; let *them* do the talking. Your job is to ask questions and listen attentively. It helps to write down a few questions before meeting with a donor.

> "John, tell me what it's been like volunteering for the past year and the impact it's had on you."

> "Jen, I heard you recently took a tour of our new offices and met the staff, what was your impression of each?"

> "Casey, what are your hopes for our seniors' program? How do you see yourself getting involved?"

If you have not yet had a chance to share your "connection story" (why you're passionate about supporting your nonprofit), do so *briefly* before moving on to "making your case." The reason why you've chosen to support your nonprofit over others can have a tremendous impact on the donor's willingness to give. Remember, personal testimonies are some of the most powerful purchasing motivators.

> "When I heard what The Hunger Coalition was doing for children, I knew I had to volunteer. My dad went bankrupt when I was 12. I had many sleepless nights because I went to bed hungry. At school, I'd mooch food from friends and tell them I forgot my lunch at home. This went on for two years until my dad got back on his feet. So my heart bleeds when I hear about hungry kids right here in Lincoln. The program staff is amazing, the chief executive spends money wisely, and

the board is engaged. Most importantly, kids in this town don't go to bed hungry, they do better in school, and graduation rates are up 22 percent in the last two years!"

3. Touch a heart as you make your case

Sometimes asking for money doesn't require a reason, you just ask. This can happen when you know a donor well, or when you've done a good job of educating a donor. Basically, you've done the heavy lifting before the ask; all that's left to do now is make the ask.

"John, would you be willing to support the new solar panel research at the same level you did last year?"

In other cases, asking for a donation is more involved. A donor may ask you to give them a reason *why* they should give you money, or you may sense a moment when you should offer a reason. This can happen at any point in the donor lifecycle, which means you should always be prepared to make a persuasive case why a donor should support your mission.

This is especially important if you're making an ask for a *specific* program, facility, camp, or whatever. You need to persuade donors why the thing you're so passionate about building, expanding, or hosting is worthy of support. Keep it brief; you don't want to bury donors in details.

Rainmakers know that the best time to make a case for support—if they feel the need to make one—is just after they've finished pleasantries. It's important to do this early in the conversation so there is plenty of time for discussion.

If a donor doesn't ask you to give them a reason why they should support you, but you feel it would improve your chances of getting a "Yes" to your ask, wait for a positive and upbeat moment in the conversation and then simply and persuasively make your case.

Always, always frame your support statement in a way that shows the needs you're fulfilling, not the needs you have. This is important because a donor must understand how the money they give you will benefit those you serve and the community—not your nonprofit.

Yes, your nonprofit will benefit too; you just want to frame the reasons why in a manner that emphasizes the work you're doing or those you're helping. Read the two examples on the next page. In Example 1, the emphasis is on the needs of the nonprofit. In Example 2, the emphasis is on the needs of the children. Which is more persuasive?

> *Example 1:* "Our weekend meal program for children is growing 20 percent a year. Our goal this year is to grow the program another 10 percent. Would you be willing to make a $3,000 donation to support our work and help us achieve our goal?"

> *Example 2:* "Last year, our program provided weekend meals to 300 children who otherwise would not have food to eat on the weekends. This year, the goal is to help 330 children—a 10 percent increase over last year.

> Plus, we'll be providing recreational and educational activities after mealtimes. A gift of $1,200 sponsors one child to have 600 meals throughout the year. That's just $2 a meal. Would you be will willing to provide weekend meals for three children for an entire year at $3,600?"

THE ASK

1. The right moment
Rainmakers know there is no perfect time to ask. They know every meeting, person, venue, and conversation is different, which means the "right moment" will vary.

However, if you're following the 3-Step Ask Process, a good time to make an ask is after the "touch a heart and make your case" stage. Wait for a relaxed moment in the conversation when you sense the donor's body language is positive, the energy between you is good, and the conversation is upbeat. When this moment arrives, make a simple and straightforward ask.

> "Dale and Megan, would you be willing to make a $5,000 donation to sponsor five children to attend the year's summer day camp?"

It's important not to wait too long to make an appeal because you'll need time to handle objections, talk about acknowledgement, express gratitude, discuss next steps, and end with pleasantries. The last thing you want to do is "rush" the end of a meeting after a donor commits to making a gift.

2. Ask for a specific amount of money, but be reasonable
When asking for money, Rainmakers ask for specific amounts because it demonstrates leadership and confidence.

First-time donors. For a first-time donor, deciding what the initial ask amount should be can be tricky. If you've done a good job of cultivating a donor, you should already know a little about their line of work, business history, lifestyle, and the sizes and types of gifts they've made to other nonprofits. If you don't know any of this information, ask your team members; perhaps they'll have some insights.

Rainmakers know that it's smart business to ask a first-time donor, especially a major donor, for a modest donation. They know that large, first-time gifts from major donors are rare because many donors like to test the waters with smaller gifts. They also know gift sizes can jump substantially if a nonprofit proves its worth and does an outstanding job of stewarding a donor after a donor makes their first gift.

> "Jim, I'm grateful for the interest you've taken in our mission to serve women of domestic violence. I know you have the capacity to make transformational gifts like the one you made for the pet center. However, today, I want to ask if you'd be willing to make a modest, first-time gift of $2,500 to support the care services of five women staying at our shelter. Then over the next year, I want to show you the impact your gift is making in the lives of our clients and in the community, and why we're a great social investment worthy of a larger gift . . ."

Current donors. If you're asking a current donor to renew their annual gift, it's okay to ask for a higher amount if it's reasonable. For example, you could increase the ask amount by 10 or 15 percent over the previous year's gift, or you could ask the donor to move up a rung on your giving ladder, or you could ask for a $5,000 gift from a donor who made a $500 gift the previous year because you know the donor has the capacity, but was testing the waters.

If you've done a good job of nurturing, informing, and engaging a donor throughout the year, and proving that you're a sound social investment, there's a good chance they will say "Yes" to your increased ask amount. If it's too high, you can bet they'll let you know.

Better yet, a driving goal of Rainmakers is to get their donors so engaged in the work of their nonprofits that they offer to donate.

> "Tom, I love what you're doing and would like donate $1,000."

When you come across a donor like this, try to ask for a bit more before accepting the offer.

"Dale, that's great. How gracious. You've been a faithful supporter and volunteer for years; I wish I could clone you! Your donation is timely because we are in the middle of a matching campaign. So let me ask, would you be willing to increase your gift from $1,000 to $1,500 if I can get two more people to match your $1,500 gift for a total of $4,500?"

3. State the specific use

Donors want to know where their money is going. By telling a donor specifically what their money is supporting, you're satisfying a major expectation donors have about the money they give. The more specific and tangible you can be, the better.

This is also the time to talk about restrictions. Most nonprofits prefer to receive unrestricted gifts, but assuming a donor wants their gift marked as unrestricted can be a big mistake. The larger the gift, the more important it is to clarify the type of restriction, if any.

> *Unrestricted funds.* These funds allow a nonprofit to use the money for any type of approved expense.

> *Restricted funds.* These funds must be used for the purpose stated by the donor or outlined by the nonprofit (e.g., a specific program or service).

> *Temporarily restricted funds.* These funds state that the funds must be used within a certain time period, or until a stated condition is met (e.g., once the YMCA's new gym is built, the donor's gift will be used to support the Y's youth basketball program).

Donors may place restrictions on their donations, so you need to have a basic understanding of the different types. Talk with your chief executive or accountant to learn more.

4. Present your giving prop (visual aid) if you are using one

One of the best tactics you can use when making an ask is to show a donor a "giving prop" (e.g., challenge table, matching gift pyramid, giving ladder, sponsorship options, wish list, etc.). These props provide a donor with a visual representation of the donation options you're offering (See Chapter 23 for examples).

Rainmakers use props because they know the likelihood of a donor making a gift increases when given choices, or when they know others are taking part in a fundraising effort, or when a competitive environment is in play. Props have the ability to transform a personal ask into a collective ask, which can make a donor feel they are part of a bigger giving picture.

Crafting an ask can be a challenging task, but with a giving prop, much of the work is done for you. It acts as a "show and tell" piece that outlines what giving levels are available, how to give, and a general reason to give—all without having to say a word. Props do much of the asking for you and provide a funding funnel for donors, simplifying the decision-making process.

When using a giving prop, it's okay to show a donor the prop as you're making the ask, but do not hand it over to them until you've made the ask. Otherwise, they may get distracted. By holding the prop, you control the show-and-tell.

A lot of creativity can go into the design of giving props. Let's say you're creating a giving pyramid for hunger relief. You could have the pyramid designed like a bowl of fruit, with each fruit worth some value, and the higher the fruit in the pile, the more value it has.

To go one step further, you could write a donor's name on the piece of fruit that's valued at $2,500. When you meet with them, show them the graphic design of the fruit bowl and a specific piece of fruit with their name written on it, along with other people who donated at that level.

Another effective tactic is to tell a donor who else you're planning to talk with that may be willing to fund you at the same level they are, especially if they know the people you plan to ask.

> "Jon, here is the challenge pyramid we've built for the Hunger Basket campaign [show them the prop]. The Petersons and Kohls are "buying" kiwi fruits at $2,500. Would you be willing to match their gift at the kiwi level?" [now hand them the prop.]

5. Stop talking and listen
Whether or not you use a prop, once you make the ask, be quiet! Shhhhh. Don't talk. Not a word. Nada. Let the ask stew. You want to create a prickly, reflective moment for the donor. The quiet tension may feel uncomfortable, but it's essential that the first person to talk after the ask be the donor.

6. Discuss the details and handle objections

Once a donor starts talking, there is no telling what they'll say. They could say "Yes" or "No," require clarification, express objection, or have questions about payment options.

Whichever direction the conversation goes, your objective is to remain composed and engage the donor in a two-way conversation to answer questions, satisfy their concerns, provide options, and agree on a donation amount. Remember, you're a philanthropic concierge and you want to help the donor achieve their philanthropic goals.

3-Step Process for Handling Objections

1. *Acknowledge.* Acknowledge the objection with empathy

2. *Options.* Provide options in an effort to find a solution

3. *Close.* Close with another ask or agree to next steps

Repeat this 3-step process until the donor agrees to make a donation, declines to make a donation, or until you both agree to next steps that may lead to a donation (e.g., another meeting, sending a proposal, meeting with the program director of the foundation, etc.). For more on handling objections, see Chapters 25-28.

THE FINISHING TOUCHES

1. Thank, summarize, and discuss next steps

The donor requests "next steps." If a donor is not ready to make a "Yes" or "No" decision once you ask for money, you'll need to take "next steps." A donor may require a proposal, request specific information, suggest another meeting, need to talk with a partner, obtain board approval, or they just may want to postpone their giving.

Regardless of their reasons for needing to take the "next steps" option, express your gratitude for their willingness to meet with you that day and give them a date when they can expect to hear from you.

If you brought a proposal or appeal letter with you, and you discussed the details of it during the meeting, give them a copy to take home. Most likely, it will require changes. Tell them you'll send a revised version in a day or two.

Follow up immediately with any other requests they asked of you and set a date to meet again as soon as possible.

The donor emphatically says "No." Not every donor will give you money. Some will give you an emphatic "No" regardless of what you say or do. When this happens—and it will—thank the donor for considering a donation and express your gratitude for taking the time to meet.

If the atmosphere is amicable, ask the donor if they would be willing to give you a reason for saying "No." Knowing their reason will give you "closure" and the feedback can help you learn from the situation.

Also, ask the donor if they are willing to accept further communications from you. Find out what methods of communication they prefer (email, written, social media, phone calls), the frequency (monthly, quarterly, annually), and the type (programs, finances). Also, ask if they would like to receive invitations to special events and volunteer opportunities.

The donor says "Yes." If the donor says "Yes" to your ask, then . . . congratulations! Express your gratitude and joy. Smile big and express your appreciation for their involvement and willingness to make a difference. After that, thank them on behalf of the board, briefly recap salient points relevant to the donation, and restate the impact their gift will have on your beneficiaries, organization, and the community.

If you brought a proposal or appeal letter with you, and you discussed the details of it during the meeting, give them a copy to take home. If there are no changes, they will have a document outlining the agreement of their donation. If the document needs modification, tell them you'll make revisions and send an updated version in a day or two.

2. Discuss gift structure and recognition
Once a donor says "Yes" to an ask, there are some structural elements of the gift you'll need to sort out.

Payment type. Ask the donor what method of payment they prefer: Credit card, check, account debit, bank transfer, Venmo, or stock transfer.

Payment frequency. Ask the donor about the frequency of their donation: single payment, quarterly payments, or recurring monthly credit card charges.

Recognition and naming. As much as you may want to leverage a donor's name, status, and gift size for credibility, publicity, or to raise additional funds, it's very important you first get permission from the donor. In fact, you should always assume you *cannot* publish a donor's name until you get permission.

To get permission, simply ask the donor how much freedom you can have to use their name in print, on the Web, in videos, and on television, and then get them to approve the suggested usage. If the donor's gift qualifies them for naming rights (e.g., buildings, rooms, programs), this may be the time to discuss the details.

The more detailed the naming rights, the more important it is to have the specifics outlined in a document that the donor signs. The process may require another meeting.

Get the correct spelling. No one likes his or her name spelled incorrectly. Misspelling a donor's name shows carelessness and can turn a donor off. It's a mistake too many nonprofits make too often.

Rainmakers always ask donors how they would like their names spelled when acknowledged in print, online, and in person. Ask regularly because the names of donors can change unexpectedly due to marriage, divorce, and death of a loved one.

For example, a donor may feel comfortable with you calling him "Jon," but for acknowledgement purposes, he may prefer "Jonathon." If a donor is separated, ask how they would like you to display their name. If you're planning on engraving a donor's name on a building, double check the spelling format with the donor and have them sign a document confirming the format.

3. Follow through
Whether the donor says "Yes," "No," or requests "next steps" to your ask, some type of follow up is usually required. You may need to revise a proposal, set up another meeting, update a pledge card, send an acknowledgment letter, invite them to a volunteer orientation party, or agree to send them your latest IRS 990s.

Whatever is required and whatever you promised to deliver, make sure you do it quickly. If you can do it within 24 hours, great! However long you tell the donor it will take, deliver on your promise and try to deliver it sooner. If you hit a snag, simply write the donor and let them know when they can expect it.

Rainmakers know one of the best ways to show a donor you value them and their donation, and that you and your nonprofit are professional and credible, is to follow up and follow through quickly and professionally.

"Always frame your support statement in a way that shows the needs you're fulfilling, not the needs you have."

CHAPTER 23

THE ASK: TYPES AND FORMS

W hat is the most effective ask type to use to raise money? That depends. What works for one donor may not work for another. Rainmakers keep it simple. They follow an ask process, like the one outlined in the last chapter, to manage the flow of an ask meeting and then choose a combination of ask types and props they feel will be most effective for the situation.

You should do the same. Learn the ask types and props below and then combine them to create an effective, strategic approach to asking your donors for money based on the setting, type of donor, and the fund-raising goals you hope to achieve.

Ask Types and Forms

1. Non-monetary ask
2. Simple ask
3. Challenge ask
4. Matching ask
5. Pyramid ask
6. Recurring gifts
7. Lead gifts
8. Giving clubs
9. Sponsorship gifts
10. Wish lists
11. Gift tables
12. Multiyear gifts
13. Endowment gifts
14. Estate gifts

1. Non-monetary ask

Rainmakers know one of the most effective types of asks you can make is one that requests a non-monetary gift. The purpose is to ask people to support your mission with whatever time, skills, expertise, favors, and influence they have to offer. This is an effective tactic because it feels "low risk" to donors, and once they get connected and involved in the work you do, it is much more likely they will support you financially when the time comes. Also see "Connection Ask" on page 27.

> "Teri, I understand your CPA firm has a nonprofit accounting division. Would you be willing to ask a few of your team members if they would review our IRS 990 before we submit it?"

> "Aaron, we are having difficulty getting our sales permit approved by the city for the "Concert in the Park" event we're hosting. As the former mayor, would you be willing to make a call to a friend or two at City Hall to see what can be done to move the approval process along?"

> "Susan, we need a decorator's touch. Would you be willing to stop by the new gym and give us some advice on how to make it look 'cool' and inviting for the kids?"

2. Simple ask

A simple ask is nothing more than a basic question you use to ask a donor for money. It's the essence of most ask types and it's made up of three components: an appeal, an amount, and a stated purpose for the funds. That's it.

> "Jen, would you be willing [appeal] to make a $2,000 gift [amount] to support the children's choir program [purpose]?"

> "Holly, would you join me in supporting the new rehabilitation wing with a lead gift of $40,000?"

> "Fred, would you be willing to sponsor four kids for a year's worth of literacy coaching for $2,000?"

3. Challenge ask

A challenge ask creates a competitive environment that encourages donors at all levels to give money to reach a funding goal. The best-known visual representation of a challenge prop is a thermometer. The more donors give, the higher the indicator moves up the thermometer.

Rainmakers use props like thermometers because they provide visual tools that encourage new giving, increase current giving, and track total giving. You can design them to work with almost any giving campaign: board giving, annual giving, program expansion, new facility construction, or during the open auction portion of a fundraising event.

Challenge asks are effective because they have a self-fulfilling element. The closer you are to achieving a challenge goal, the easier it can be to fulfill it (which can boost your confidence as well). Why? People like to win, achieve goals, and be part of a team that wins by achieving its goals by specific deadlines.

This is why it's important to create some type of prop to visually represent the progress of your challenge ask campaign—people want to see how close they are to reaching the goal and winning!

You don't need to use a thermometer as your prop, but whatever you choose, it should be creative, ignite a competitive spirit, and be prominently displayed, even publicly if possible. You should also put a graphics version of the prop on your website.

> "John, with two weeks left in our annual 'Plant More Trees' campaign, we've raised $75,000 of the $100,000 goal, as you can see by our redwood tree graphic here [show graphic prop]. Would you be willing to buy a 'Branch' for $5,000 in an effort to help us fill out the entire tree with branches by the two-week deadline?"

> "Peggy, I want to thank you for visiting the soup kitchen today. You now see why it's important we expand the warehouse if we're going to feed more children. The Madisons and Crafts made $1,000 gifts last week. Would you be willing to match their gifts and make a $1,000 gift so we can fill the breakfast bowl [show graphic prop] and reach the $30,000 expansion goal by June 1?"

4. Matching ask

A matching ask is a form of a competitive ask where you tell a donor that if they are willing to make a gift, you're confident you can find one or more donors who would be willing to "match" their gift.

Rainmakers like using matching asks because they know donors become very motivated to give once they realize they're in a competitive environment (especially with friends and peers), where they can be part of a collective effort to achieve a financial goal to support a worthy mission by matching the gifts of others. In fact, a matching ask campaign can increase overall giving by 30 percent.

Matching asks are also versatile. You can include a matching ask tactic with almost any ask type. Once you have one donor committed to a gift you can go to other donors and try to find matching gifts, no matter what ask tactic you're using. Or, if you have multiple donors committed to making gifts, you can go to one donor and ask them to match the collective gifts of others.

There are many ways to craft and use matching asks and props. They are very effective fundraising tactics so whenever possible, think of ways you can frame an ask in the form of a match, or use it to augment other types of asks.

> "Adam, if you're willing to make a $10,000 gift, I'm confident I can find two more donors who would be willing to match your gift."

> "Sherry, we have seven people committed to giving $2,500 to support our new program. Would you be willing to match their gifts with a gift of $2,500?"

> "Wiley, the Jenz Foundation is willing to make a lead gift of $1.2 million if we can raise $500,000 in next 60 days. The Spauldings are committed to $100,000. Would you be willing to match this gift if I can get three more people to match yours?"

5. Pyramid ask

Gift pyramids provide donors with giving alternatives in an easy to understand visual format. At a glance, donors can see all the available choices and decide which level or block they want to fund or sponsor. The higher up the pyramid, the more expensive the block.

Rainmakers like pyramid props because they provide elements of a competitive ask and a matching ask. You can ask donors to "buy" squares to complete a level or achieve a fundraising goal. You can incite donors to give at higher levels than they did the year before, and you can ask donors to match giving levels of other donors.

In most cases, each pyramid block not only represents a dollar figure for how much you want to raise, but how many people you want to give at that amount. For example, at Level 2 in your pyramid, you may be looking to raise three gifts at $5,000, at Level 4 you may be looking to raise two gifts at $10,000, and at Level 5, the top of the pyramid, you may be looking for just one gift of $25,000.

Once a donor buys a block, ask if you can put their name on the block they bought. This can stir the competitive spirit of other donors you're asking and it generally increases the total amount of money you raise.

> "Peggy, you've been one of our most generous donors. Without you, we wouldn't even have a program for children. I asked you to see our soup kitchen today because I wanted you to see the impact we're having on kids and why it's important for us to double our capacity in the next two years. To do this, the kids need your help. I have a sponsorship pyramid here and I want to know if you'd be willing to take a $2,500 square?" [point to a $2,500 square in the giving pyramid that's in the shape of a dinner table]
>
> Or, "I'm hoping you'd like to sit at the table [point to the picture of the $2,500 square]. This is where I would like you to consider giving. What do you think?"
>
> Or, "Here's the size of gift I made [point to a $2,500 square in the pyramid]. I hope you'll match me and five other donors who bought $2,500 squares. Will you join us?"
>
> Or, "You probably recognize many of the names at the $2,500 level on this pyramid [point to all the names at the $2,500 level]. One more name here fills the entire row. Would you be willing to join these folks with a $2,500 gift and help us fill the $20,000 row?"

6. Recurring gifts

A recurring gift is one that's broken down into smaller increments and made at regular intervals over time. This is a Rainmaker favorite for donors who give $12,000 or less a year. Donors who say "No" to a one-time gift of $500 or $10,000 gift will often say "Yes" if you structure the gift as a monthly credit card payment of $42 or $833, respectively.

Many donors like this option because it syncs better with their cash flow, eliminates the "one big check" syndrome, and allows them to earn bonus points on their credit card.

You can set up recurring payment systems using credit cards, debit cards, automatic bank withdrawals, and payment systems like PayPal. Credit cards have expiration dates, so it's important to create a system that reminds people to update their card information when their expiration draws near. When it's time for a donor to renew a gift, create incentives for them to uptick their gift by 10 or 15 percent.

A recurring gift works best when it's tied to a particular outcome so the donor can see how you're using their donation and the specific benefit it provides.

> "Your monthly gift last year was $200. This allowed 20 blind women the opportunity to learn how to type and use computers to get jobs. This year, would you be willing to help 25 blind women by increasing your monthly gift to $250?"

7. Lead gifts

A lead gift is a very large donation that one or more major donors make to kick off a fundraising campaign or event. The purpose of a lead gift is to inspire others to join the giving initiative. A lead gift can be substantial in size, sometimes as much as 50 percent of the total goal, though 10 to 20 percent is more common.

Many major donors feel honored when asked to make a lead gift, which can deepen their emotional connection to a mission and their personal involvement to fulfill it. Lead gifts can also motivate donors to get their friends, family, and business associates involved.

Rainmakers use lead gifts because they know major donors like to see their gifts leveraged by encouraging others to give. In fact, a large gift by a well-respected donor can add tremendous credibility to a campaign and inspire dozens of people, sometimes hundreds, to follow their lead and make a gift.

When launching a campaign, talk with a few of your largest donors and ask if they'd be willing to make a lead gift. Be sure to tell them how you plan to leverage their names and gifts, and how you plan to recognize them.

> "Stephanie, as you know, we are expanding our facility to build a new recreation center for disadvantaged youth. You've been one of our most loyal supporters. Without you, we wouldn't have our current facility. In June, we are kicking off a building campaign to raise $2.5 million. On behalf of the board and all the disadvantaged children of Simi Valley, we are graciously asking if you would make a lead gift in this campaign in the amount of $500,000 . . .
>
> . . . If you make this gift, I'm confident Sam and Betty Johnson and Brandon and Cheryl Mazzi will both commit to gifts of $250,000. I'm also confident that we can leverage your name and reputation in all types of media, communications, and public appearances to raise

funds from hundreds of our donors to achieve this Herculean goal. Stephanie, will you kick off this campaign to help hundreds of children and inspire others to give by making a lead gift of $500,000?"

8. Giving clubs

Giving clubs, also known as "giving societies" and "sustainer programs," provide donors options to give at varying donation levels. Rainmakers like giving clubs because they can inspire donors to migrate to higher giving amounts over time. They also create donor "stickiness" by creating a sense of community and culture that encourages people to join a club and remain loyal to it.

If you want to use giving clubs, make sure you design them in a manner that appeals to your donors' sense of status and style, matches the themes of your fundraising efforts, and fits your culture.

For ideas, search out the largest nonprofits on the Web. Organizations like the Red Cross, The Nature Conservancy, and World Wildlife Fund use giving clubs. Also check out hospitals, universities, and large cultural nonprofits such as museums and art institutes. You can get great ideas from others who have forged ahead of you.

Some classic giving club examples include: President's Club, Director's Club, Legacy Club, Founder's Club, Founder's Society, and Heritage Society. Let's say you ran a marine preserve. You could create a set of giving club levels like these: Whale $10,000, Porpoise $5,000, Sea Otter $1,000, Penguin $500, and Starfish $100.

The possibilities are endless. Your goal is to use giving clubs to build loyalty and inspire donors to migrate to higher and higher club levels. You can only do this if you make each club something exclusive and appealing—something people feel the *need* to belong to.

For props, you can design logos, collateral material, and swag for each level. Ask yourself how you can make each level unique and special.

"Mrs. Jones, you've been a loyal Penguin giver for three years. Would you like to take a jump in the ocean and become an Sea Otter donor this year for $1,000?"

"Kenny, on behalf of the board, we're grateful for your longtime financial commitment and your dedication as a volunteer. As you know, the aquarium is under expansion. Would you be willing to make a stretch commitment and move from the Porpoise level of giving ($5,000) to the Whale level of giving ($10,000) for the next three years to fund the new 'Living Reef' exhibit?"

"Teri, we've started a Founders Club. It requires an annual gift of $5,000 and a commitment to sponsor a table at the gala for $5,000. You've been a loyal donor for 10 years and it's an honor to ask you to join this club. Would you be willing to join me in making this commitment?"

9. Sponsorship gifts

Sponsorship gifts provide donors a vehicle to underwrite specific needs of a nonprofit. For example, a donor could give $10,000 to sponsor 10 children to attend a summer day camp, or $2,500 to sponsor the backdrops of a theatrical play, or $1,000 to sponsor a child to learn how to read.

Sponsorship gifts are another Rainmaker favorite because they know donors like to give money to specific, tangible items that are measurable and often visible. What areas of your programming, operations, and fundraising can you turn into a sponsorship opportunity? Think out of the box. Have donors sponsor accounting fees, utility bills, mortgage payments, or a fundraiser. When you do create a sponsorship, make sure you develop a compelling message to entice people to "buy" it.

"Jenny, for $2,500 you could sponsor a blind, wounded warrior to attend a weeklong rehabilitation trip in Idaho to learn how to fly fish, ride horses, waterski, and kayak . . . what do you think . . . would you be willing to sponsor a wounded warrior for this camp?"

"Tim, thank you for joining me for the tour of our new tech labs for inner-city children. It costs $10,000 to sponsor a lab, which covers all equipment, educational materials, and instruction for a year. Sponsorship also includes name recognition on a plaque on the door. Would you be willing to sponsor a room for a year?"

"Sherry, we already have three commitments from other donors to underwrite this year's gala, including your best friends, Pam and Ron Selby. Would you and Jim be willing to sponsor the other quarter of the cost with a donation of $5,000?"

10. Wish lists

Wish lists are simplified versions of sponsorship lists. They provide donors (usually small- to medium-sized donors) opportunities to "buy" specific, fairly inexpensive tangible items to support a nonprofit. A wish list could include items such as program equipment, phones, shelving, a used van, and printer toner. Nothing is too outlandish to list.

Rainmakers use wish lists because they know many smaller donors are often leery of making unrestricted gifts because they are unsure where their money is going. But with a wish list item, a donor knows exactly what their donation is supporting and the benefit it will provide. It's something they can see and touch—something real.

You can also use wish lists to motivate donors to spend money at events and galas, or on your website. As you'd expect, they are very effective during the holidays. When you create a wish list, be sure to design it to look upscale and exclusive.

Wish List Example

$3,000:	3 iPads for mobile staff
$2,500:	5 office desks for interns and volunteers
$1,500:	8 food barrels for perishable food pickup
$1,200:	Gas and electric utility bills for a year
$750:	75 backpacks for children
$500:	New snow tires for "Kids Rock" van
$250:	Educational toys for children's nutrition class
$150:	New vacuum cleaner for children's playroom
$125:	New sink faucet in children's bathroom

"Hi, Val! I'm calling to see if you received the wish list I sent. Last year you bought new rugs for the Learning Center for $400. This year would you be willing to buy snow tires for our "Kids Rock" van for $500?"

11. Gift Tables

Gift tables outline how many donors you need at certain giving levels to achieve your overall giving goal. For example, let's say you wanted to raise $100,000. A $100,000 gift table would highlight how many donors you think it would take at various giving levels to achieve the goal: $10,000 (3), $1,000 (20), $500 (50), $250 (100), etc. Gift tables are typically built in spreadsheet, matrix, or infographic table formats.

You can use a giving table to help you determine specific fundraising strategies for various levels of giving within a gift table. For example, you may have a strategy to meet with major donors in face-to-face settings for gifts of $1,000 or more. You may establish a "call-a-thon" to contact people who have the potential to give between $100 and $500, and you may set up email, text, and mail campaigns for those who will likely give less than $100.

Gift tables are effective tools to help you manage your fundraising efforts, but Rainmakers often use them as props during ask meetings. They will show a donor a table that outlines the details of a particular fundraising campaign and how many donors it will take at various levels of giving to achieve the stated goals. Then they ask the donor to give at a particular level in the table.

> "Mr. Jones, you can see in this table [show the gift table] that we need 10 donors at the $5,000 level and 5 donors at the $10,000 level to achieve our fundraising goal. You've been a longtime supporter at the $7,000 level. Would you be willing to make a stretch gift this year at the $10,000 level so we can reach our goal of $250,000 by the end of June and begin construction of Cane Creek's first child vaccination clinic in July?"

12. Multiyear gifts

A multiyear donation is a commitment by a donor to make a donation each year for a given number of years. The number of years and the amount of the donation may vary. For example, a donor may commit to a $250 gift each year for three years. Or, a donor may commit to a three-year gift and give $250 the first year, $500 in year two, and $1,000 in year three.

Rainmakers use multiyear asks because they know it's an effective tactic to get donors to make long-term financial commitments. Many times multiyear asks are made in the form of pledges.

If you do a good job stewarding a donor in the first year of their pledge, and they have been engaged in your work, you may want to ask them to increase their pledge amount for the remaining years of the pledge.

> "Stan, on behalf of the entire board and the children we serve, we're grateful for the $1,000 gifts you've made the last three years toward your five-year $5,000 pledge. You've also been one of our star volunteers. I don't think you missed one event all year. You've seen the changes we make in kids' lives more than anyone and know our work is essential to the safety of children in the community. Stan, would you

be willing to increase your annual gift from $1,000 to $2,000 for the last two years of your five-year pledge?"

13. Endowment gifts

Endowments are typically "permanently restricted" donations that allow donors to make gifts to support a nonprofit, or a specific program, service, or project operated by a nonprofit. In most cases, the principal (or "corpus") of the endowment is invested, and the interest, or some portion of the investment returns, are used to fund projects.

Rainmakers like to offer endowment gifts (when available) to major donors because they know many wealthy people like to make gifts that can provide long-term recurring income to a nonprofit.

> "Marcia, thank you for the extremely generous $20,000 gifts you've made for the last four years. The entire board, staff, and all our students extend their gratitude. As you know, we are in the middle of a three-year, $1.0 million endowment building campaign for our literacy program. We have commitments from four other donors at $30,000 a year for three years. Would you be willing to match these gifts and donate $30,000 a year for the next three years?"

14. Estate gifts

Estate gifts, also known as "planned gifts," are contribution commitments made during a donor's lifetime with the benefits of the gift becoming available to a nonprofit at a present or future date. Rainmakers like estate gifts because they can provide substantial long-term financial benefits to a nonprofit and to a donor. Nonprofits typically suggest estate gifts to major donors and older donors, but they can benefit any donor.

There are many types of estate gifts: charitable trusts, gift annuities, charitable lead trusts, remainder annuity trusts, and life insurance. The details of estate gifts can be complicated because there are legal and tax implications. If you're a small nonprofit, you probably don't have the expertise to manage estate gifts, which is why it's cost-effective to partner with an estate planning professional.

The professional's job is to educate you on how to integrate estate gifts into your fundraising program and to handle the details and paperwork once a donor decides to make a gift. This means you get all the benefit with little effort.

Your job is to promote estate gifts. You can provide estate gift options in literature, at events, and on your website. "If you're interested in learning more about planned giving options, check the box below and we'll give you a call." Small call-to-action reminders like this can trigger a response from a donor when they feel the time has come for them to address estate planning.

Four out of five estate gifts are bequests, most of which are set forth in wills, but 70 percent of people don't have wills. Also, older couples without children are five times more likely to leave a bequest than couples with children. Knowing this, you may want to send out a questionnaire asking donors if they have wills, or if they have an interest in learning more about wills and estate giving.

If the response is good, host a workshop and have a financial planner talk about wills and estate planning. Make sure it's super fun, interesting, and not too long; no one wants to attend a boring workshop.

Quick tip: Serving delicious food and desserts is always a good draw.

"Create more matching gift opportunities.
Donors become very motivated to give
once they realize they're in a competitive environment."

CHAPTER 24

THE ASK: POSITIONING TACTICS

No matter what ask types and props you use to raise money, you can improve the effectiveness of your ask with a variety of positioning tactics. Think of positioning tactics as marketing strategies that influence the way donors perceive and respond to your asks. There are many different types of positioning tactics, but here are eight Rainmaker favorites.

Positioning Tactics

1. Make it easy, keep it simple
2. Ask for a modest gift first
3. Find commonality
4. Give them a reason
5. Create a sense of urgency and scarcity
6. Create a sense of exclusivity and rarity
7. Offer a social "bargain"
8. Demonstrate value

1. Make it easy, keep it simple

Many donors lead busy lives. The last thing they want to do is get bogged down in long-winded asks, mounds of paperwork, and cryptic proposals. No matter how you ask for money, make the process of giving easy and convenient. If you complicate it, a donor's passion for the mission—and for giving—may turn into irritation.

Think clarity and simplicity for every part of the giving process. Accept all forms of payment. Take credit cards over the phone, on your website, and on your smart phone. Set up recurring methods of giving. Accept stock transfers. Minimize all types of paperwork. Keep ask pitches short. Write brief appeal letters. Create easy-to-read collateral.

The more mindful you are of making giving easy, the more enthusiastic your donors will be to give.

2. Ask for a modest gift first

It was stated earlier, but it's worth repeating again: One of the smartest things Rainmakers do when asking a first-time donor for a gift, even if they are wealthy, is to ask for a modest gift. Doing so sends a message that you respect them and their money.

If you do an outstanding job nurturing your relationship with the donor, and you show them what an outstanding job your nonprofit is doing to make an impact with the modest gift they gave you, they'll be much more receptive to making a larger gift when the time comes.

> "Mr. Shuster, I know you have the ability to make a large gift, like the one you made for the YMCA last month, and I want to prove to you over the next year that we are worthy of a gift that large. At this time, I would like to ask if you'd be willing to support our Meals on Wheels program, the one you volunteered for last week, with a modest first-time gift of $2,000?"

3. Find commonality

The positioning tactic of "commonality" is a favorite among Rainmakers because they know donors are more willing to give if they feel like-minded donors are supporting the programs and mission.

For example, if you're asking a woman for a donation, share stories of what other women gave and why they gave. If you're asking a company for a sponsorship, share stories and endorsements of other companies that bought sponsorships and why they gave. If you're talking with seniors, share testimonials of other seniors who gave.

> "Karen, let me show you a short video of other professional women who tell stories of why they volunteer as mentors and financially support the "Girls Grow Strong" program [dialogue ensues after the video] . . . Each $5,000 gift sponsors 10 girls for a year. Would you be willing to sponsor 10 girls?"

4. Give them a reason

Donors have many choices. Why should they support your mission? What makes you better than the nonprofit across town that has a similar mission? Should they have a personal responsibility to help fulfill your mission?

A donor's decision to give is rooted in varying degrees of emotion, reason, and values. However, as the donation size increases, the element of reason often plays a larger role because a major donor's philanthropic equity is at stake. They want to be sure their substantial social investment will be a good one. When meeting with a donor, try to find one or two reasons that would help them *logically* justify why you're a good social investment.

> "Paul, the number of adopted children who go to college is 75 percent greater than children who don't get adopted . . . and every $3,000 you give helps place a boy or girl like Steve and Amber [show picture] in a stable household where they can study and play sports in a safe and caring environment, and greatly increase their chances of attending college. On a broader scale, an increase in college enrollment also helps break the cycle of poverty and substance abuse, and the impact on the welfare system . . ."

5. Create a sense of urgency and scarcity

Major retailers are savvy marketers. They use classic positioning tactics like urgency and scarcity to sell products because they know it motivates consumers to act quickly and buy, and they know if their customers fail to act, they will feel like they missed out on a great deal.

Rainmakers like to use these same tactics because they're powerful motivators for major donors. Wealthy people are often quick to buy when they know there is a *limited time* to buy a new car model, a membership to a private country club, or tickets to a Super Bowl game.

They are also quick to buy when there is a *short supply* of something such as a vintage Bordeaux wine, front row seats to a concert, reservations at an exclusive restaurant, or an oceanfront condo.

In essence, when you tell a donor you're trying to raise a specific amount of money for a specific reason by a specific deadline, you're telling them that what they are doing is important, demands attention, and requires immediate action. This is why a challenge or matching ask with a deadline is so powerful.

If you use the positioning tactic of urgency or scarcity, make sure that it doesn't sound like you're desperate for money.

> "Liza, we're trying to make our budget for the year. If we don't reach our goal by June, we may have to cut back our educational programming at the community garden. Can I count on you for a gift of $2,500?"

This type of frantic and distressed ask may work once or twice, but you run the risk of losing future donations because it sends caution flags that your nonprofit may be mismanaging funds. Here are some better options:

Availability scarcity. "We have one week left to reach our goal!" "There are only three $2,500 spots left on our 'Build Homes for the Homeless' giving pyramid." "The first 10 donors who give $10,000 receive four free tickets to the opening performances of our three ballets this year."

Programming scarcity. "We're the only nonprofit in the country helping blind wounded veterans learn how to snowboard."

Sponsorship scarcity. "We have only two children left to sponsor at $1,000. After that, we have $1,500 sponsorships."

Time scarcity. "Our 'Raise Up a Child' campaign ends in six days. Would you be willing to donate $500? If you do, we will be only $4,000 short of our one-month goal of raising $20,000."

Time scarcity. "Heidi, we are only $2,000 short of our $40,000 goal. We are trying to raise the remaining $2,000 by this Saturday. Would you be willing to match your last year's gift of $1,000? If you commit today, I have another donor who will match the gift by tomorrow."

6. Create a sense of exclusivity and rarity

Many major donors live in a world of privilege and exclusivity. They belong to country clubs, tennis clubs, and yachting clubs. They eat at fine restaurants, get special car detailing, visit expensive spas, and travel to exotic destinations. And some have multiple homes, custom clothing designers, and a private jet.

Knowing this, Rainmakers often think of ways to position their asks in a manner that takes advantage of a donor's desire for exclusivity.

"Mrs. Cohen, we are only having one lead gift for this year's gala. We would be honored if it were you. Would you be willing to make a lead gift of $100,000? Before you answer, let me tell you we have two other donors willing to make $25,000 gifts and we're confident we can raise an additional $150,000 during the live auction. We will also give you stage-side seating next to comedian Eddie Murphy. The following night, we've arranged a private dinner with five other donors and actor Tom Hanks, who is one of our supporters. What do you think?"

Or, "We know this is a substantial gift, but we are only asking three people to give $100,000. Your family has been supporting us for three generations and we're grateful. For your gift, we want to do an exclusive article in this year's impact report thanking your family for all the support your family has given The Hunger Coalition over the years."

Or, "You are the only donor I'm asking to make a lead gift and be a featured speaker at this year's wine auction. Your support and willingness to speak at the fundraiser will inspire and motivate dozens of our top donors to follow your lead as we work to raise our first million dollars for The Hunger Coalition."

7. Offer a social "bargain"

Everyone likes to feel they are getting a deal when buying something—even donors. This is why real estate agents often show potential buyers the more expensive homes first. It's also why giving pyramids, challenge gifts, and gift ladders are so effective, and why Rainmakers often position an ask as a bargain because they know it entices donors to give at the bargain amount.

For example, let's say your objective is to secure a $1,000 donation using a giving pyramid. The first thing you would do is show the donor one or more larger options, knowing that your target is $1,000.

"Ryan, as you can see on this year's Founder's Club giving pyramid, we have a wide range of support levels starting at $5,000 [point out the $5,000 and $2,500 levels and then pause for a few seconds]. You can breathe easy though because I'm not going to ask you for a gift at these levels. Instead, would you be willing to consider a gift at the $1,000 level?"

8. Demonstrate value

Everyone wants a bargain, but Rainmakers know smart donors care just as much about value as they do about price. A seasoned donor isn't going to give $1,000 to a shoddy nonprofit instead of giving $2,000 to a high-performance nonprofit just because the appeal is $1,000 less.

Rather, a seasoned donor, if given a choice between similar nonprofits asking for the same amount of money, will typically give to the nonprofit they feel provides the best value.

Because "value" is a relative term, it will vary from donor to donor. Some donors may be motivated by financial value. Some may be motivated by program impact value, and some may be motivated by board value, management value, growth value, or competitive value when compared to other nonprofits with similar missions.

Your job is to discover what type of value will motivate a donor and then craft an ask to incorporate it.

Impact value. "Stacy, let me show you how your $2,500 donation will provide lunch meals for 50 children for an entire year—that's just $50 per child."

Comparison value. "Stacy, let me show you how your $2,500 donation can feed 30 percent more children than the hunger relief organization across town."

Management value. "Stacy, our executive built three other nonprofits similar to this in the last 10 years. She has a track record of raising substantial sums of money and building winning program teams. When I think of the management value you get with Karen and her team, I can't think of a better investment."

"Keep the giving process simple.
If you complicate it,
a donor's passion may turn into irritation."

CHAPTER 25

OBJECTIONS:
AN OVERVIEW

Rainmakers know objections are part of the ask process, which is why they embrace them. There are dozens of reasons why donors throw red flags and the next few chapters provide a process, a handful of guiding principles, and set of practical tactics you can use to transform those red flags into green ones without losing hope.

Kick the tires

Let's say you walked into a Chevy dealership and the sales manager stepped up, smiled, and said, "How would you like to write us a check today for $75,000 to buy this new Chevy Tahoe?"

Even if you loved the vehicle and were interested in buying it, you'd likely have a number of questions you'd like answered before you wrote a check and signed the paperwork. You may want to talk about payment options, body style, and feature options. You may want to compare the SUV to competitive brands, and you'd certainly want to talk it over with your partner.

Like buying a car, making a donation is an important financial decision for most donors. Therefore, Rainmakers *expect* and *anticipate* questions, concerns, and objections as part of the ask process.

A donor may be thrilled with your mission and excited to financially support it, but before they write a check, especially a big one, you may need to answer some questions and address their concerns. They may want to look under the hood, kick the tires, review the warranty, and go for a test drive. That's understandable, right?

In fact, if a donor isn't asking questions and doesn't have concerns, you may want to consider asking for more money!

The chances of a "Yes" aren't good—they're great!

Before you start worrying about all the different types of objections and how you're going to deal with them, remember this: If you've done a good job of cultivating and stewarding your donors, they won't have to kick the tires and go for a test drive, and there is a good chance they will say "Yes" to your ask.

As you recall, the chances of getting a "Yes" to an ask can be greater than 70 percent, sometimes greater than 90 percent, depending on the donor and their level of passion and involvement. With odds like this, it's easy to be confident.

However, there will be many times when a donor hesitates or objects, or says something like "Yes, but . . ." because something about the ask isn't quite right—the amount, timing, payment schedule, restrictions, area of funding, etc.

Hiccups like these might be an inconvenience, cause a little stress, and stall the process, but once you work through the things that are causing a donor to balk, chances are very good they'll make a donation.

Prepare yourself for objections—design a process
Okay, objections are inevitable; you get that. What's probably making you anxious, and what makes many people anxious about handling objections, is thinking you need a scripted response to address every type of objection.

This is a futile task so don't waste your time trying. A more effective strategy, and the one Rainmakers use, is learning and applying a simple *process* for resolving objections (next chapter). You'll still need to develop a few rehearsed responses to the most common objections, which you'll learn, but then you'll be set. With a little practice and experience, you'll quickly have the confidence you need to handle nearly any objection.

Besides the responses you'll learn in *Cloudburst,* you should hold brainstorming sessions with your team members to come up with objections your team is likely to encounter, based on the types of asks they plan to make. The team can then prepare and practice objection responses to refine its objection handling skills and increase everyone's chances of getting "Yes" responses.

Team members can test each other by asking "what if" statements. "What if the donor says the amount of the ask is too much?" "What if the donor doesn't want to give to the food basket program?" "What if the donor says they can't give until the economy gets better?"

Never strong-arm a donor

No matter how good or bad the ask process is going, *never* strong-arm or guilt a donor into a donation, especially after a donor objects. If you do, you may get a donation, but it may also be your last. Donors loathe pushy and controlling fundraisers.

Worse yet, if a donor feels strong-armed or manipulated during the ask process, they may tell their friends about it at the next social function they attend. This will likely taint your brand and negatively impact donor giving. This is why it's imperative to be respectful, forthright, and grateful when asking for money, no matter what the situation.

When a donor hesitates or objects, it doesn't mean "No"

Now, if you've done your homework, established a relationship with a donor, and a donor gives you a meeting, you're in good shape—they're interested. So when they hesitate or object after you ask for money by expressing some type of concern, it doesn't mean they are explicitly saying "No." "No, I have no intention of making a donation."

Rather, in their mind, they are probably saying some form of "I'm interested, but . . . ." "I'm interested, but I have a concern about timing." "I'm interested, but the amount is too much." "I'm interested, but I have a few questions." "I'm interested, but I need to pay my taxes first." "I'm interested, but I want to support your other program."

As a Rainmaker, your job is to expect and anticipate these types of objections and be prepared to address them, and then continue to walk the donor through the ask process until they say "Yes," "No," or agree to next steps.

When a donor objects, it's not a personal rejection

Let's be honest, any response other than "Yes" from a donor when asking for money can be emotionally unsettling. Why? Because we fear rejection. We fear we might not be able to answer a donor's questions. We fear we won't be able to turn an objection into a "Yes."

Any type of objection or any form of "No" can make us feel like we are *personally* being turned down. Asking someone for money can produce a similar feeling a person gets when asking someone out on date for the first time. It produces a lot of anxiety and worry for fear of being turned down (rejected). Therefore, to protect our pride and remain comfortable, it's safer not to ask in the first place.

Even worse, if a person is brave enough to ask someone for money and then is turned down, it can squelch their confidence and motivation, and discourage them from asking anyone else for money.

These are realistic fears and concerns that people exhibit when asked to raise money. There is a good chance that you and your team members experience these feelings. That's okay; there are ways to combat them.

First, if a person genuinely fears fundraising and has no desire to learn or try, then they should NOT be forced to fundraise. No one should ever be forced to raise money! If they are, the nonprofit risks losing donors and income through unsavory experiences, and losing staff and board members who would rather resign than be forced or coerced to raise money.

On the other hand, if people have a willingness to raise money, then there are many ways to help them confront and work through their fears and anxieties, and teach them how to become happy, effective, and fearless Rainmakers.

If you're one of these people, the three most important things you should focus on to help you overcome your fear of asking people for money are education, preparation, and practice (See chapter 37).

Once you learn what to do, how to do it, why you're doing it, and then practice doing it, your comfort and confidence levels will climb, your fears and anxiety will lessen, and more and more donors will say "Yes."

Another tactic you can use to help you reduce your anxiety is to remind yourself that you are not asking people for money to help *you*. Rather, you are simply a conduit, a messenger, asking people to support an issue or mission *they* believe in.

So if they support your mission, great! If not, it's not because of you or what you said, or what you didn't say. It's their decision, no matter what the reason.

The circumstantial "No"

If you have a good relationship with a donor and they've been engaged and faithful, and you're able to make an ask in a face-to-face meeting, and they say "No," there's a good chance it's circumstantial.

> "I've been laid off."
>
> "Our son was recently diagnosed with leukemia and we need to prepare for an avalanche of medical costs."
>
> "I'm going through a difficult divorce."

When you hear responses like this, it's important to validate a donor's situation and show them you care by expressing compassion and patience.

One thing you can do is ask the donor how they would like to remain connected to your nonprofit. Perhaps they would like to remain on your email list and your event invitation list. Give them some space. When the time is right and their circumstances change, they'll return, and when they do, they'll respect you for respecting their situation.

The casual "No"

No matter how well you prepare, no matter how well you nurture your donors, and no matter how well you handle objections, some donors will say "No" when you ask them for money. It's inevitable and it's okay. Not every new donor will want to support your mission. Not every current donor will want to continue supporting your mission.

A donor has the right to say "No" whether they give you a reason or not. Rainmakers respect this right. When a donor finally says "No," express your gratitude for the opportunity they gave you and then ask them how they would like to remain connected to your nonprofit, if at all.

As you walk away, smile and remind yourself you are a kind and passionate person doing the best job you can to help a worthy mission. You're a Rainmaker! You're *proud* to ask people to support your mission—whether they choose to or not. Wipe the dust from your sleeves, pick up the phone and call the next donor.

The emphatic "No"

In the rare situation where a donor emphatically says "No! . . . I want nothing to do with this organization . . . take me off all your mailing lists and don't ever call me again!" When this happens, be calm and polite.

Thank the donor for considering your nonprofit, exit graciously, and honor their request.

If possible, find out why the donor is so emphatic about not supporting you. If they are willing to respond, be kind, considerate, and listen patiently. Do not be defensive. Why? Because if you say or do something offensive, you run the risk that they may tell their friends.

It's important to protect your personal and corporate image. Let the donor vent and exit gracefully. Then quietly move on. There are many other donors to contact who are eager to give.

Demanding and rude donors – when you say no!
Rainmakers know that some donors can be controlling, rude, snobby, picky, disrespectful, annoying, and downright obnoxious. Some donors believe they should be able to influence how you run programs if they make a substantial donation. Other donors feel their donations entitle them to make outrageous demands, claim a board seat, or expect special attention and coddling.

Even if a donor has good ideas or intentions, it doesn't mean you should act on them. Most donors have no idea what a headache their suggestion would cause if you implemented it. As the fundraising adage goes "Don't change your mission in order to ring the register!" This means there will be times when *you* need to tactfully push back and say "No."

When you run across high-maintenance donors, you need to develop strategies to manage them. The best way to do this is to be honest and polite with them early on about what they said, how they made you feel, or what boundary they crossed.

But no matter what they said, did, or proposed, never offend or fight with a donor. Your public image is worth big money and it's important you protect it at all costs.

Yes, donors will make good suggestions to improve programming. Yes, donors will expect special treatment. Yes, donors will be rude and inconsiderate. But your job is to let donors know the personal and organizational boundaries you have in place and to do it in a gentle and respectful manner.

Example 1

[You] "Hey John, I know you'd like us to send you monthly updates on giving, but we would have to pay our bookkeeper additional funds to do that. The board recently cut our bookkeeper's hours to keep administrative costs down. We send out statements quarterly, I hope that works. If you have specific questions between statements, just call me; I'd be glad to answer your questions over the phone."

Example 2

[Donor] "Tom, I've called your office three times and no one can seem to give me a straight answer. What's going on over there? If your staff can't even field a call correctly, how can I trust that they're going to manage my donation wisely?"

[You] "Mr. Peters, I can understand how you feel. I would be upset if the same experience happened to me. You did the right thing by telling me about your experience. I'll talk with the staff supervisor as soon as we get off the phone. Our administrative staff prides itself on providing first-rate customer service, so it surprises me to hear about your experience. I do know they are short staffed right now because two interns went back to college. But that doesn't matter. Good customer service, means good customer service . . ."

"Never strong-arm or guilt a donor into a donation.
If you do, you may get a donation,
but it may also be your last."

CHAPTER 26

OBJECTIONS: 3-STEP PROCESS

Y ou will encounter objections when asking donors for money. It's a given. As discussed, one tactic for handling objections would be to develop and memorize a response to every possible objection. Rainmakers know this is an ineffective approach because a donor can give dozens of responses (objections) to a single ask question, which is what makes asking for money so nerve-wracking for most novice fundraisers.

A more effective approach, one Rainmakers use, is to learn a *process* for handling objections that you can apply to any objection.

Below is a three-step process for handling objections. Simply repeat the process until the donor agrees to make a donation, declines to make a donation, or until you agree to next steps that may lead to a donation (e.g., another meeting, sending a proposal, observing a program, seeing construction plans of a proposed facility, etc.).

3-Step Process for Handling Objections

1. *Acknowledge.* Acknowledge the objection with empathy

2. *Options.* Provide options in an effort to find a solution

3. *Close.* Close with another ask, or agree to next steps

1. Acknowledge the objection with empathy
When a donor objects to an ask, the first thing you want to do is acknowledge their objection—with empathy. This validates a donor's right to object by showing them that you've listened, you care, and you're clear about their objection.

Keep the acknowledgement short. Maintain a sincere and empathetic tone. If you neglect to acknowledge a donor's objection, or try to defend your ask, or push for a donation, you will turn off the donor and lose the donation, and possibly the donor.

"I understand this month might not be a good time . . ."

"I can understand how you might feel . . ."

"I agree, the economy is rough right now . . ."

"I can appreciate the position you're in . . ."

"I recognize that $5,000 is a lot to ask . . ."

"I sense that the timing is not good for you . . ."

"I can identify with what you're saying . . ."

2. Provide options in an effort to find a solution

After acknowledging an objection, you'll want to provide one or more options to help the donor overcome their objection. Rainmakers know when you provide donors with options, when you find solutions to their concerns, you transform "Yes . . . buts" into "Yes . . . that works!"

Let's say you're talking with a donor who objects to your ask because they don't want their donation to cover administrative costs. In this case, you could provide them with the *option* to make a restricted gift to a particular program or service.

You could also make the case that your programming and services would not be able to exist without administrative functions and that your administrative costs are far less than the national average and those of your competitors.

Quick tip: Getting major donors to cover administrative costs will increase giving by minor donors who are often turned off by such costs.

When all options fail, use "Donor's Choice"

No matter how many options you provide, sometimes you just can't find one the donor likes. When this happens, it's time to ask probing questions such as "May I ask why you're hesitating?" "May I ask what's causing you to object?" or "What's on your mind?" Questions like these can get a donor talking to reveal what's in their heart or on their mind.

However, when a donor has balked at two or more options, it's time to turn the tables and provide *them* a chance to make a suggestion. Rainmakers call this option "Donor's Choice."

"Wayne, it sounds like you want to support us, but I need your help here. What do you suggest we do to make this work?"

"Kim, what can The Hunger Coalition do to make this work for you?"

Once you hear a donor's response to questions like these, and it's positive, which it usually is, you have a starting point from which you can shape an ask or a close that creates a win-win.

3. Close with another ask, or agree to next steps

After offering a donor various options to overcome their objections, three results are imminent: They will say "Yes," "No," or you will have to take some form of "next steps."

1. **Yes.** If a donor says "Yes," express your gratitude and thank them for the gift. Next, you'll want to talk about payment options and acknowledgment. And last, you'll want to talk about next steps (e.g., follow-up paperwork, meetings, introductions, volunteering opportunities, etc.).

2. **No.** If a donor says "No," make sure you've offered enough options, including a "Donor's Choice" option. You'll also want to confirm the donor's "No" is not circumstantial due to a job loss, divorce, tax liability, etc. If it is, grant the donor grace and ask how they would like to keep in contact until the timing is better.

   If it's not circumstantial, ask the donor if there is anything you can do that might change their mind. If it's clear that the donor doesn't want to make a donation, graciously thank them and ask if they would like to remain on your email recipient list for events and updates. Also, ask if it's okay to call on them once a year.

3. **Next steps.** If a donor says "Maybe" or is unsure about their donation intentions after you've provided a number of options, then it's best to wrap up the meeting and talk about next steps. The next steps might include a meeting with the donor's partner, an updated proposal, a tour of the facility, or a call with the board chair.

   Whatever it is, graciously thank the donor for their time and act quickly to set in motion the next steps.

> "It's smart business to ask a first-time donor, especially a major donor, for a modest donation."

CHAPTER 27

OBJECTIONS:
TACTICS FOR COMMON TYPES

Rainmakers know the majority of objections they face when making an ask revolve around two responses: 1) The amount of the ask and 2) The timing of the ask. The tactics you'll find in the following pages will help you overcome these common objections and a few others.

As for the dozens of other types of objections, don't worry; if you learn the tactics on how to handle the objections in this chapter and the next, and apply the basic process of handling objections you learned in the last chapter, you'll have all the confidence you need to handle any rare and unusual objections that come your way.

Objection: The ask amount is too high
Tactic: Spread it out, break it down

One of the most common objections you'll hear from a donor is that the amount of the ask is too high. Donors have budgets for giving, cash flow limitations, and asset restrictions, and if you ask for too much money, a donor is likely to object.

The Spread it Out, Break it Down tactic is a favorite among Rainmakers to address this objection because it eliminates the single-payment option that often burdens donors. Instead it creates a set of smaller payments (monthly, quarterly) a donor can pay over time, therefore, allowing a donor to "spread out" their gift.

Example 1

Ask
[You] "Would you be willing to give $1,000 to support our new swimming program?"

[Donor] "I'm sorry, but $1,000 is way too much money for me."

Acknowledge, Option, Close
[You] "I can understand. If someone asked me for $1,000, I wouldn't be able to give it all at once, either. How about this . . . to create a better fit

for your cash flow, what if we spread out the donation by breaking it down in to four quarterly gifts of $250, or a monthly gift of $83?"

[Donor] "Terrific! I like the $250 a quarter option—that would be perfect."

Example 2

Sometimes the amount of your ask will be too high no matter how you try to spread it out. In this case, reduce the gift amount by 25 percent and then ask the donor if the new amount, as a single-payment, will work. If they say "No," offer them the option of spreading out the newly reduced amount.

If the donor says "No" after two gift amount reductions, offer them a Donor's Choice option (See page 117).

Ask
[You] Would you be willing to give $1,000 to support our new swimming program?"

[Donor] "I'm sorry, but $1,000 is way too much money for me."

Acknowledge, Option, Close
[You] "I can understand. If someone asked me for $1,000, I wouldn't be able to give it all at once either. How about this . . . to create a better fit for your cash flow, what if we spread out the donation by breaking it down into four quarterly gifts of $250, or a monthly gift of $83?"

[Donor] "Sorry, but that's still too much money for me . . . I just can't afford to give $1,000."

Acknowledge, Option, Close
[You] "Okay, no problem. I understand. However, I have a suggestion that might be more in line with your budget. Would you be willing to give $600 to sponsor three kids for summer swimming lessons?"

[Donor] "Yes, I'd like to do that, and it's more in line with what I was thinking."

[You] "Would you like to make a one-time gift of $600?"

[Donor] "Do you have any payment options?"

[You] "Yes. Let's set up the gift as a $600 pledge. What works best for you, four quarterly gifts of $150, or 12 monthly gifts of $50?"

[Donor] "I like the $150 a quarter option; let's do that."

A note on pledges

When Rainmakers feel a donor is unwilling to commit to an ask, they often provide the option of making a pledge. By getting a donor to agree to a pledge, you're getting a "Yes" to your ask *and* you're allowing a donor to make a donation when it's financially convenient for them. It takes the pressure off you and the donor. It's a win-win.

A pledge tactic is basically a different form of a Spread it Out, Break it Down tactic. The primary difference is that you're using the term "pledge" when talking to the donor about deferring a single-payment, or how to spread out their gift over time.

If you use the pledge tactic, it's important to know that pledges, when structured as such, are often considered legal contracts. Talk with your accountant to determine your state's position. Most pledges are fulfilled, but a nonprofit has the right to take legal action against a donor who defaults on a pledge, though this rarely happens.

Regardless, you should take a best practice approach and specify the terms of any pledge or deferred payment option in written format (letter or email). The letter should state the amount of the pledge, amount and frequency of payments, start and end dates of payments, any restrictions, and any other important items discussed with the donor.

To further complicate matters, the Financial Accounting and Standards Board (FASB) now requires nonprofits to report pledges on their accounting statements as a way to show all assets and resources. This means you'll have to work with your bookkeeper and accountant to ensure your books accurately reflect future financial commitments made by donors, whether you classify them as pledges or some type of promise to pay—including commitments you secure from donors using the Spread it Out, Break it Down tactic.

As a final thought, you may want to consider using the pledge tactic as an ask tactic, not just when overcoming an objection. Rainmakers know many donors are willing to give more when asked for a gift in a pledge format because they know they can pay the gift over time, like a car lease. Think of ways you can design pledge packages that encourage donors to make stretch gifts.

Objection: The ask amount is too high
Tactic 1: Reduce the amount using Feel, Felt, Found

The "Feel, Felt, Found" tactic is an age-old sales tactic that fundraisers adopted decades ago. The basic premise works like this: You acknowledge a donor's objection and validate their position by expressing empathy, and then you offer an alternative option based on personal experience.

Rainmakers like this tactic because it's easy to remember and apply, and it has a proven track record of success. Practice it a few times on team members and you'll see how easy it is to learn.

Ask
[You] Would you be willing to give $1,000 to support our new swimming program?"

[Donor] "I'm sorry, but $1,000 is way too much money for me."

Acknowledge
[You] "I can understand how you might *feel* a $1,000 gift is too much money right now. I was asked recently for a $1,000 gift by the YMCA and *felt* the same way. Like you, I said, 'I can't afford that right now.' But when they reduced the gift size and asked if I would be willing to make a $700 gift, I *found* that I could make a gift."

Option and close
[You] "Would you feel comfortable making a gift of $700?"

[Donor] "Sure, Tom, that would work."

Thank you and next steps
[You] "Great! On behalf of the board and all the kids in the swimming program, we're grateful for your support. I know you like to make gifts online, so I'll send you an email with a link to our online donation page when I get back to the office."

[Donor] "Yes, that would be fine. Thanks, Tom."

Objection: The timing is bad
Tactic: Spread it out, break it down

A donor may have the ability to give $1,000, but maybe you asked at a bad time. They may be facing an unexpected expense such as a divorce settlement, tax liability, tuition bill, or down payment on a house.

Bad timing is a common objection and here are some other responses you can expect to hear: "Some changes have come up, I can't make a decision right now." "I need to discuss this with my (partner, trustees, or CEO)." "I just made a large gift to another organization." "I need to think about it for a while." "We're going to wait until next year."

Rainmakers know small and medium-sized donors tend to make donations based on their available cash and income. Major donors often have more predictable giving patterns because they establish giving budgets and know with a fair degree of precision how much money they plan to give at specific times throughout the year.

Either way, if the timing of your ask comes at an inconvenient time, no matter what the reason, it will impact your ability to get a "Yes" to your ask. Therefore, you need to come up with options to timing objections, like those in the following paragraph and in the examples below that put you in a position to receive money when a donor has the capacity to give money.

"Yes, life can be hectic. When would you like me to follow up?" "What month is best to talk with you about the proposal we'll be submitting?" "Important decisions take time, and we are happy to hear that you will give this opportunity serious consideration." "I can certainly understand that you'd want to talk this over with your CEO."

Example 1

Ask
[You] "Would you be willing to support our children's food basket program with a gift of $1,000?"

[Donor] "I'm sorry, Tom, this is a bad time. I just paid my quarterly taxes and I don't have that kind of cash to give away."

Acknowledge, Option, Close
[You] "I understand. Last year I was hit with a large and unexpected tax liability, and if someone had asked me for $1,000, I would have said, 'Not now, the timing is terrible.' Consider this: To create a better fit with your cash flow, what if the donation was spread out over a year, broken down into four quarterly gifts of $250, and the first gift wasn't due for three months?"

[Donor] "Wow, now that would be great! Let's do it!"

Example 2

Sometimes the amount of money you ask for is too much *and* the timing is bad. In this case, you'll need to provide options that reduce the amount of the ask and adjust the timing.

Ask

[You] "Would you be willing to support our children's food basket program with a gift of $1,000?"

[Donor] "I'm sorry, but $1,000 is way out of my range. I don't make gifts of that size, and the timing is bad; I just paid an unexpected tax bill."

Acknowledge, Option, Close

[You] "I understand. Last year I was hit with a large and unexpected tax liability, and if someone would have asked me for $1,000, I would have said, 'Not now, the timing is terrible.' Consider this: To create a better fit with your cash flow, what if the donation was spread out over a year, broken down into four quarterly gifts of $250, and the first gift wasn't due for three months?"

[Donor] "Wow, that's a nice offer. But $1,000 is too large a gift no matter how you slice it."

Acknowledge, Option & Close

[You] "Okay, I understand. How about this . . .Would you be willing to sponsor six kids to receive food baskets for a year for $600? I can set it up so you can make quarterly gifts of $150 starting in three months."

[Donor] "Perfect. Let's do it!"

Objection: The donor offers to make a small gift

Tactic: Upsell the gift by finding middle ground

You know the donor. You've done your homework. The donor has given $2,500 the last three years. You make an ask of $2,500 this year. The donor responds that they would like to make a gift of $1,000. Whoa! You're shocked. How do you respond?

There will be many times when the amount you ask for and the amount a donor expects to give are different. Rainmakers don't simply accept a donor's offer. Instead they try to "upsell" the gift by finding middle ground. You can do this by encouraging a donor to consider a gift that is 20 to 50 percent above the offer they made.

You can also use the Spread it Out, Break it Down tactic to create an attractive giving option that syncs with the donor's financial position. Or, if you're using a gift ladder or a giving pyramid, you can ask the donor to consider giving at a higher level than the one they chose.

The goal here is not to try and strong-arm the donor into a bigger gift. The goal is to tactfully test the waters to see if the donor is willing to make a slightly higher gift. You'll find that 50 percent of donors will say "Yes" to a higher gift after they've announced the size of gift they would like to make.

Ask

[You] "Sue, you've been a loyal supporter of our community garden for three years. Would you be willing to continue your support at the $2,500 Founders Club level?"

[Donor] "Tom, please understand, I'm a huge fan of the garden, but this year I'm going to make a gift of $1,000 instead of $2,500."

Acknowledge, Option, Close

[You] "Thank you, Sue! That's very generous. You're not only one of our most loyal supporters, you're one of our best volunteers. Let me show you this graphic that highlights our new giving levels. At $1,000, you'll become a "Giving Tree" member. The next level up, at $1,500, is the "Sustainable Farmer" level. At this level, you qualify to receive one free basket of fresh produce from the garden each month. Would you be willing to support the garden at the "Sustainable Farmer" level?"

[Donor] "Sure, why not . . . and I'm thrilled about the idea of receiving fresh produce!"

Objection: The donor stalls and wants to think about it
Tactic: Let the donor think about it

Rainmakers know some donors, especially major donors, will not make a decision on the spot. They will gladly meet with you, talk about giving options, and express sincere interest in donating. However, before deciding, they want time "to think about it."

A response like this should come as no surprise because making a donation for some donors is a serious decision, no matter what the gift size. Also, a donor may need to consult an accountant, financial planner, family members, or board members before making a decision.

Therefore, never rush a donor. Exercise restraint and patience, and give donors adequate time to make giving decisions, which may require a blend of follow-up calls, emails, and face-to-face meetings. If you are patient with your donors, they will be gracious to you.

Ask
[You] "Kip, would you be willing to make a $10,000 gift to support the expansion of our women's shelter?"

[Donor] "Let me begin by telling you that our family would enjoy making a gift to support the new expansion. A $10,000 gift is a reasonable ask and I think the family would approve it, but I need to run it by our board of trustees next month."

Acknowledge, Option, Close, Next Steps
[You] "No problem. I understand. Would you like me to write up a one-page appeal letter outlining the details of the gift?"

[Donor] "That would be great. Thank you."

[You] "I'll email it to you tomorrow. I'll also make a note in my calendar to contact you in mid-October to follow up. We can set up a call or another meeting at that time to discuss the gift. Will this work for you?"

[Donor] "Yes. Perfect."

One more example!
Here's one more example. Can you spot the three steps of the ask process and the three steps of the objection process?

[You] "Hi Peggy! I'm so glad you could join me today to see our new soup kitchen in action and lend a hand. Serving food to so many young children really makes your heart sink, doesn't it? What were you thinking and feeling while helping today?"

[Donor] "Mostly, Tom, I was shocked by how many children you serve and how young they are—preschoolers for goodness' sake! Some looked happy, others looked hopeless. I had to do everything to hold back my tears when those second grade twins walked through the line."

[You] "As you know, Peggy, our goal is to help the parents of girls like Holly and Amber move from a state of dependency to self-sufficiency through self-development. If we accomplish that, hundreds of children like Holly and Amber can eat at home, not here."

[Donor] "Yes, I'm learning more and more that the root of hunger is poverty, not just lack of food. That lesson was clearer than ever today."

[You] "Well, as you can see, we've just completed building this amazing soup kitchen that can serve 150 people an hour. Also, as I said earlier, we've doubled our job-training program for single mothers so we can serve 100 women every six months. The women leave with valuable skills to secure good wages. About 80 percent of the women who go through our training programs get jobs within 30 days and 60 percent of these women keep their jobs for two years or more."

Peggy, we're grateful for the $5,000 gifts you've been making each year, but this year, would you be willing to make a stretch gift of $7,000 . . . $3,500 to help us pay off our kitchen equipment loan and $3,500 to sponsor 10 women to attend our 10-week job training program?"

[Donor] "Tom, that sounds great, but I only budgeted $5,000 again this year."

You: "I understand. I have a set budget for my giving too. What if I said you can make one payment of $3,500 now, $2,000 in June, and $1,500 in December? Would that work?"

[Donor] "Yes, I can do that."

[You] "Thank you, Peggy! I'm so grateful! It's people like you that really help make a difference in the lives of children like Holly and Amber and their mothers. You help in so many ways, not only as a volunteer, but also with all the referrals you've made and your help with the Full Plate gala. What a blessing you've been . . .

I'll write up a pledge letter outlining the payment schedule and email it tomorrow. It will state that the donation will equally support the soup kitchen and jobs program. I'll send it tomorrow. How would you like to make your first payment—check or credit card?"

[Donor] "Credit card."

[You] "That's fine. I'll send you an email with a link to our donation page so you can make your gift online like you did last year. For the last several years, we've announced your gift in the newsletter and annual report; would it be okay to do that again this year?"

[Donor] "Sure, no problem."

[You] "And you'd like to use your formal name, 'Margaret Smith', right?"

[Donor] "Yes, thank you."

[You] "Peggy, I think a testimony from someone like you would inspire others to give. Would you be willing to write a three-sentence testimonial about why you support us? I plan to publish it on the website and in our impact report along with a photo of you."

[Donor] "That's fine. I would love to help."

[You] "Wow, you're an amazing woman with a huge heart for helping those in need. I wish I could clone you! Your gift will help many kids like Holly and Amber so they don't go to bed hungry and their mothers can acquire the skills they need to get good jobs so they can care for their children and live independently. Thank you so much!"

[Donor] "You're very welcome. It's a pleasure supporting such a worthy mission."

"If you are patient with donors,
they will be gracious to you."

CHAPTER 28

OBJECTIONS: TACTICS FOR UNCOMMON TYPES

You've heard it chapter after chapter: If you do a good job of cultivating and stewarding your donors, the chances of them saying "Yes" to your ask can be greater than 70 percent, and in some cases greater than 90 percent. If a well-prepped donor does balk, getting a commitment is usually just a matter of working out a few details.

Those attempting to raise money without properly preparing donors are likely to hear more objections because they've missed the big picture—the *process* of raising money. Their donors tend to have less trust, less connection to the mission, and less loyalty—therefore, less interest in giving.

Rainmakers understand that the process of donor cultivation and stewardship is the key to fundraising success. However, no matter how long you've been raising money and how well you nurture donors, you're sure to encounter objections, and some will be quite odd.

This chapter covers a few of the less common objections you may encounter and a set of tactics you can use to overcome them. If you're properly managing your donors, many of these objections will come into play long before you ask for money, which means they should no longer be stumbling blocks at the time of the ask.

No matter what type of objections come your way, remember this: Unless you get a flat out "No, I don't want to make a gift of any type" response to an ask, there is *always* hope you can find a solution that leads to a "Yes." Your job is to inject creativity and grit into the process of finding a solution, and if you run out of ideas, offer up a "Donor's Choice" option (see page 117). You can't go wrong with that.

Objection: The donor gives to other nonprofits

Sometimes donors have money to give, but they are apprehensive about giving it to you. They may not know much about your nonprofit. They may already be giving to another nonprofit with a similar mission, or they may not trust your nonprofit.

The tactic here is an ongoing process of education and familiarity. Develop ways to inform donors about what you do, why you do it, and how your nonprofit is more effective than the ones across town. Get donors involved in some small way so they can see firsthand the difference you're making and why you're a worthy social investment. Ask for a very modest first-time gift, or a non-monetary gift.

> *People say:* "I'm already giving to an organization like yours."
>
> *Your response:* "That's great. There are many nonprofits helping the hungry. What I'd like to do is ask you for a modest gift now and then show you throughout the year why we're a high-performance nonprofit making unprecedented changes in the lives of impoverished youth."
>
> *People say:* "I give to too many organizations right now."
>
> *Your response:* "I understand this must feel overwhelming. There are many high quality organizations in the area. Let me just say, we have many donors like you who make gifts to multiple nonprofits. Here's what I'd like to propose . . . I would like to ask for a modest gift of $500. Then over the next year, I want to show you why so many of our donors who support multiple charities make us their top choice. Let me explain a few of the differences that make us stand out . . ."

Objection: Use of funds

Donors can be very picky about where their money is going. Some refuse to have any of their money support administrative expenses. Others only want to support their pet programs and projects. Suggestions to the contrary are met with apprehension and discontent.

When Rainmakers run into situations like these, they try to make a case of why it's important for donors to support the entire organization or the project in question. However, if they encounter strong resistance, Rainmakers acquiesce to the donor's desire because they know it's better for a donor to be joyful and support areas of a nonprofit that interest them rather than have them give to something they are not excited to support.

> *People say:* "I don't want to give to the afterschool lunch program; I want to support the soup kitchen."
>
> *Your response:* "We use the soup kitchen to feed the kids that attend the afterschool program, so by supporting the soup kitchen, you are supporting the afterschool program. Let me give you some other examples that show the connection between the programs . . ."
>
> *People say:* "I don't want any of my money to go to administrative expenses."

Your response: "I can understand your concern. A number of nonprofits around town have exceptionally high administrative costs. Only 10 percent of our funding goes to administrative costs. This is far below the national average of 40 percent. Plus, without therapists on staff, we wouldn't have any programs. Let me walk you through our administrative expenses so you can see how we spend our money . . ."

People say: "I'm sorry, I don't want to make a second gift this year to the capital campaign because I only want to support the new ballet program and I only want to make one gift a year."

Your response: "I can understand. However, the building is very old and if we don't make the required improvements, the city will force us to close. That means no ballet! We're grateful for your current gift of $1,000. Would you consider matching that gift to support the building repairs?"

Objection: The Economy

Personal finances affect personal giving. So when the economy dips and a donor's wealth shrinks, their charitable giving usually shrinks as well. A major downturn in the economy can be a valid reason for not making a donation, but some donors use it as a scapegoat. "I would like to give, but this economy is making it so I can't."

When faced with an objection centered on the economy, Rainmakers focus on the needs of their nonprofits and their beneficiaries, not the economy, and offer gift options that allow a donor to spread out their donation over time.

People say: "It's a tough economy; I think I'll wait and see once things turn around."

Your response: "It *is* tough out there!" In fact, demand for our homeless services goes up when the economy tanks. In the last 100 days, it's doubled. How about this: What if I spread out your $1,000 donation over the next year by breaking it up into 12 monthly gifts of $83. Plus, I'll set it up so you don't have to make your first gift for 60 days."

People say: "I can't make a donation at this time. The economy is in a slump and so are my finances. I'm just not in a good position to make a $1,000 gift."

Your response: "Believe me, I understand. The economy has pinched everyone's pocketbook. However, your participation will help those who are standing in soup lines to get the food they need *and* job placement assistance so they can find work and become self-sufficient—even in this economy! With this in mind, would you be willing to renew your annual $1,000 gift if it were broken down into three gifts, the first of which wouldn't be due for four months?"

Objection: I'm unemployed

No matter what the reason, when people lose their jobs, regardless of how much they were making, they can feel financially "poor." This can cause people to restrict giving in an effort to retain their money.

Rainmakers know the best strategy to use here is to acknowledge someone's plight and then ask if they're willing to continue giving at a lower rate. If not, wish them luck finding a new job and then tell them you'll call back in six months. Make note of their job situation in their profile.

When you call back, be prepared to hear that their job status has not changed. If this is the case, do not ask for a gift; share some lighthearted stories about the good work your nonprofit is doing and then tell them you'll follow up in six months. However, if they have found employment, move tactfully forward with a modest ask.

> *People say:* "Sorry, I'd like to give, but I can't—I recently lost my job."
>
> *Your response:* "I'm very sorry to hear that. We're not going anywhere. I'll tell you what; I'll call back in six months. Meanwhile, focus on yourself and your family and I hope you find an even better job than the one you had. Sound good?"
>
> *People say:* "We're in the middle of corporate restructuring. We had to layoff 20 staff and we're cutting back on all expenses, including charitable giving. I don't think we'll be making any charitable gifts for at least a year."
>
> *Your response:* "Wow, I'm so sorry to hear that. I'm sure it's a tough time for everyone at Crafty Software. You've been loyal supporters and we don't want to lose you. Let me talk with my team; I'm sure we can grant you some grace so you can retain your sponsorship status with us while things settle. Showing the community your continued support of seniors will be good for your public image. As for renewing your sponsorship, well, we can talk about that later this year, okay?"

Objection: Damaged goods

Nonprofits of all sizes make mistakes and bad decisions. A serious blunder can negatively impact the image of a nonprofit and cause donors to reduce or stop their support.

A major donor should never learn a piece of earth-shaking news from a source other than from you. Therefore, if your chief executive gets fired, your bookkeeper embezzles funds, a board member violates a conflict of interest policy, or a child gets hurt due to a negligent act, you'll need to do damage control to retain donors and keep your brand shiny.

When a *major* tragedy strikes, the kind that's sure to leak to the public, like embezzlement, it's important to quickly and transparently address the issue and discuss how you plan to deal with the problem. Call your major donors. Send letters and emails to your other donors. Also, get the media involved so they can inform the community.

You must take decisive action and aggressively define your position. Otherwise, gossip will define it for you—and that's never good.

For smaller tragedies, like when a staff member speaks rudely to a donor, or you've done a terrible job stewarding a donor, take quick action to make amends with the donor. Meet with them in person if possible. Allow them to vent their frustrations. Listen without judgment. Be patient. Don't defend. Find ways to help them feel that their issue has been resolved so they can move past it and remain a loyal supporter. It's all about providing exceptional customer service, so do it exceptionally well.

> *People say:* "I'm sorry, but I'm not donating this year. I donated last year and had the worst donor relations experience ever. No one thanked me for my gift, my gala invitation went to my ex-husband, and the development officer only calls me once a year—when he needs money."
>
> *Your response:* "I'm so sorry; that's very disrespectful and unprofessional. If I were you, I'd be just as upset, if not more so. You're a loyal and major supporter, and I feel awful you had such a terrible donor experience. I will be sure to talk with the staff about this immediately. As the chief executive, I will gladly be your primary contact going forward and I promise you'll have a first-class donor experience in the coming year . . ."
>
> *People say:* "I've heard you have some serious board drama going on over there . . . yelling, disengagement, and people resigning. I don't want to support a nonprofit whose board is so dysfunctional."
>
> *Your response:* "Yes, we had some board drama. But that's all behind us. The slate has been wiped clean. We have a new board chair and we replaced seven out of nine board members. The new board is deeply engaged and it is committed to taking the organization to new heights. We have a donor meet-and-greet next week and I would like you to attend so you can meet board members and see for yourself just how authentically passionate they are . . ."
>
> *People say: "I don't like my contact person."*
>
> *Your response:* "I'm sorry to hear that. You've been a longtime supporter and faithful volunteer of the soup kitchen, and we want you to be happy and continue your support. It's important to have a contact person you like and trust. Knowing how much you like sailing, I think Peter

Stam would be the perfect board member to work with you. In fact, I think his wife plays tennis in the same league as your wife. I'll set up a meet-and-greet between you and Peter and you can let me know how it goes. Sound good?"

People say: "I heard about the embezzlement scandal. How can I trust you now?"

Your response: "Yes, our bookkeeper embezzled money. It's very embarrassing. In response to the situation, our board members are giving $10,000 of their own money to reimburse the organization to cover the $8,000 that was taken. Also, we have a new bookkeeper in place and we've instituted new accounting procedures that were created by the city's largest accounting firm."

Another response: "What happened was terrible, but our programs were unaffected and we're helping more children with autism than ever before. The situation was a blip in what we consider a stellar track record of great management and wise use of funds. I'm asking you to consider continuing your support for the 1,000 things we've done right, the hundreds of children your contributions have helped, and the enjoyment you get out of volunteering, instead of rejecting us for the one thing we did wrong."

"Donors are busy.
If they feel you are wasting their time,
you will get less of their time, and money, in future."

CHAPTER 29

THANKING AND RECOGNITION

For many nonprofits, getting the donation defines fundraising success. They get the "Yes," high-five the success, send out a generic tax letter, and move on to the next ask. The donor's name slips to the back of the list and they don't hear from anyone for a year. The result: The donor feels neglected, sometimes used, and reduces their gift or stops giving.

> "More than 40 percent of nonprofits do not send a thank-you note after receiving a donation."

Rainmakers know that successful fundraising is a year-round activity that resets itself with the thank-you process. They also know one of the most important factors determining whether donors make second gifts is how they were treated after they made their first gifts, which is why Rainmakers take exceptional care to make donors feel valued and appreciated during the thank-you process.

Create a thank-you and follow up process
To thank donors efficiently and effectively, you'll need to create a formal *process*. The system doesn't have to be complicated, but it does need to be systematic and consistent. Otherwise, donors will slip through the cracks and you'll eventually lose them and their future gifts.

The type of thank-you process you develop will depend on your resource capacity. If you have a total of 50 donors, you should send handwritten notes and make phone calls to everyone after they make a gift. If you have 3,000 donors, a staff of five, and a board of six, you'll need to develop a much different process.

The five-step process on the next page is a simple but important one. It's designed to thank major donors after asking them for money in face-to-face settings, though you could use it to thank donors of any size. If you don't have a process in place, it's a good one to model.

5-Step Thank You Process

1. Tell the board and key staff
    Within 24 hours
2. Write one or two handwritten thank-you notes
    Within 1 week (48 hours is best)
3. Phone calls
    Within 2 weeks (1 week is best)
4. Send an IRS acknowledgment letter
    Within 3 weeks
5. Follow-up customer service call
    Within 4 weeks

1. Tell the board and key staff
Timeframe: Within 24 hours

A large gift from a major donor is big news. When you receive one, send an email announcement to members of your team, the board, and staff. Doing this is not only a good way to share the news, it's a great opportunity to validate the hard work everyone is doing to support the mission and your fundraising efforts.

When you hit major fundraising milestones, or receive an exceptionally large gift you've been working months to secure, throw a small party to celebrate and share the excitement.

2. Write one or two handwritten thank-you notes
Timeframe: Within 1 week (48 hours is best)

Donors get plenty of junk mail and long-winded letters from financial advisors. Rainmakers know long and boring form letters get skimmed or tossed in the trash. One of the best ways to thank donors is to send thank-you notes. Never email thank-you notes unless requested to do so by a donor, or unless your donors know that you're trying to reduce paper waste.

Send two *handwritten* notes within the first week of receiving a gift—one by the person who made the ask and one by a board member, staff member, chief executive, or beneficiary. The note should be sincere and personal. Let the donor know they've done something wonderful, something pivotal. You are not only thanking the donor; you are congratulating the donor and celebrating the difference their gift will make.

Encourage everyone to write clearly and legibly. Use simple, everyday vocabulary. If the handwriting of a board member looks more like hieroglyphics than a note, have a staff member transcribe it. If you want to score big points, include a powerful photo in the card. Or, have custom "photo cards" made that showcase the work you do and the people you serve. Design the cards in a manner that leaves space to write a thank-you note. And use a font size people can read! – 13 or 14-point.

Not everyone is a prize-winning writer, so to improve the quality and impact of your thank-you notes, have one or two of your star writers create a few samples. Those who will be writing thank-you notes can use the samples to get ideas as they craft their thank-yous.

If you feel you must send a thank-you form letter along with handwritten notes, make it personal, thoughtful, and brief. Try to refer to the donor by name at least twice. Emotionally connect them and their gift with the work they're supporting. Choose a classy layout design, write short paragraphs, and use generous amounts of white space.

Quick tip: Send a "welcome kit" along with a thank-you note. The kit can provide a calendar of events, ways to get involved, and key information.

Example

Handwritten note from a board member:

> Jim and Susan:
>
> Thank you for your gift of $5,000. It will allow 10 girls to attend our summer day camp program for foster children. Gifts like yours are critical to the development and happiness of all the girls we serve. Imagine the lasting change you'll make in these girls' lives after they've spent a week with mentors who love them and empower the girls to make wise and healthy decisions.
>
> We're thankful for your loyalty and it's been a joy for the girls and the counselors to have Susan volunteer as a mentor.
>
> With gratitude,
>
> John Smith, Board Member
>
> P.S. I've included a picture of the camp you sponsored last year. I love this picture; it warms my heart and puts a smile on my face every time I see it. Girls in Motion is making a difference and your support helps make that difference a daily reality for the girls you're supporting.

3. Phone calls

Timeframe: Within 2 weeks (1 week is best)

Within two weeks of receiving a gift, make at least two thank-you calls if it's a major donor, one or two calls if it's a mid-level donor, and one call if it's a minor donor (if you don't have too many of them). Board members, team members, and the person who secured the gift are obvious choices of people to make the calls, but staff members, volunteers, committee members, and honorary members are also good choices.

Your brand is on the line every time you talk with a donor so choose people who *want* to make calls and are good at it. Don't force people to do it. A lifeless thank-you call sounds disingenuous and invalidates the donor and their gift. To add significance to your thank-you calls, have a beneficiary, a parent of a beneficiary, or a celebrity make one of the calls.

Write sample scripts and share them with callers. Change the scripts frequently to keep the messages fresh. Encourage callers to keep calls brief—just a couple of minutes. If the donor wants to keep talking, that's fine, but it's important for the caller to respect the donor's time.

The caller should graciously and enthusiastically thank a donor for their gift and express what the gift means to the work of the nonprofit, the people it serves, and the community. Let the donor know that you look forward to their involvement and hope to see them at upcoming events.

Quick tip: Don't leave a thank-you message on a donor's phone until you've tried calling three times. For the first three calls, leave a message stating your name, organization, and that you'll be calling back, or that they can call you at the number you leave. If you've been unable to connect by the fourth call, leave a thank-you message of the type outlined in the paragraph above.

4. Send an IRS acknowledgment letter

Timeframe: Within 3 weeks

The IRS requires that all donors who make donations over $250 must receive notice that they made a gift. This notice is usually sent in the form of a letter through the postal service or in an email. Many nonprofits send an acknowledgment notice no matter what the gift size.

Send the notice within three weeks of receiving a gift. The IRS requires the letter include the statement "No goods or services were made in exchange for the gift" if that statement applies to the gift.

You'll also want to include a section stating the terms, amount, and date of the gift. If necessary, include a section stating what the gift was supporting, any restrictions placed on the gift, and how the funds will benefit the beneficiaries, organization, and the community.

The letter should include a few brief statements thanking the donor for their gift and the impact it will have. The chief executive is usually the person who signs the letter. The bottom of the letter should include a handwritten postscript to further personalize the letter and express gratitude. Always use high quality paper stock to give your letters a professional look and feel.

At the end of the year, it's a good idea to send a "donation summary" document listing all the donations a donor made throughout the year. There are also donor management systems that allow nonprofits to create cloud-based profiles where donors can fetch acknowledgment letters and year-end giving summaries.

5. Follow-up customer service call
Timeframe: Within 4 weeks

This is an optional call. The purpose of this call is to ask the donor if they received their IRS tax letter and any follow-up materials they were expecting to receive. It's also a chance to ask about their giving experience and to let them know that someone from the volunteer team will be contacting them if they expressed interest in getting involved.

However, if you've already made two thank-you calls to the donor, you should not make this call because three calls in a month may annoy them. A better option is to combine many of the customer service components listed above into your second thank-you call but wait to make the call until a week or so after you've sent the IRS acknowledgment letter.

Many fundraisers miss opportunities to say thank you because the opportunities are not obvious or they are not a priority. On the next page are a few tactics you can use in less obvious situations to express your thanks and show supporters why you're grateful.

New and different thank-yous

Times are changing. Handwritten thank-you cards will remain a classic, but there are many new ways of saying "thank you" to donors. Below are a few Rainmaker favorites, but you should brainstorm with your team members to come up with a few of your own. Think of small, novel, and affordable things you can do to make your thank-yous stand out from the traditional thank-yous most nonprofits send out.

1. Take a donor to lunch with a beneficiary

2. Honor a donor at a special event

3. Make dinner for a donor (a Rainmaker favorite)

4. After receiving an online gift, send the donor a link to a thank-you page or a thank-you video

5. Create a personalized thank-you video

6. Send a birthday card or anniversary card

Board member thank-yous

Most nonprofits require their board members to make annual gifts. Unfortunately, because these gifts are viewed as "requirements," many nonprofits don't have a process in place to thank its members for their gifts. This is a mistake. It's important to thank members regularly, not only for their financial contributions, but also for their contributions of time, expertise, influence, and volunteer work.

Set up a system to thank board members in writing, on the phone, and in person. If you want your thank-yous to feel especially meaningful, thank your members publicly. You can thank them at a member dinner, annual retreat, major fundraising event, or public outreach event.

Foundation and corporation thank-yous

When thanking foundations and corporate sponsors, you can do a lot more than thank the organizations for their gifts. Take time throughout the year to thank the *people* who helped champion your proposal or sponsorship. Make calls and handwrite personal notes. Invite them for a site tour or take them to lunch.

In your impact report, or other public areas of recognition, set aside areas that allow foundations and corporations to stand out separately from donors. To win the hearts of your funders, send a poster-sized framed photo of your beneficiaries or the work you do. It should be classy, something they'll be proud to display. Handwrite a clever note of gratitude on the bottom: "Your support changed our lives! Thank you for the best summer camp ever! . . . [signed] Kids Beating Cancer."

Rainmakers do the small stuff to thank people because they know it's people who support their nonprofits, not foundations or corporations.

Pledge thank-yous
Some nonprofits only send one thank-you notice after receiving a multi-payment pledge no matter how many payments it is. Rainmakers thank donors who make multi-payment pledges each time they receive a payment, even if it's monthly. They know it's a good way to update donors on the status of their pledge and to "touch" them on a regular basis with news and information, and ways to get involved. How often are you thanking your multi-payment donors? What can you do or say to express your gratitude?

Thanking the deceased
How do you acknowledge someone if they die in the year they made a donation? You write a gracious note to the family acknowledging the donor's contribution and the impact their contributions have had on your beneficiaries, organization, volunteers, and the community.

If you have a good picture of the donor with a beneficiary, or working as a volunteer, frame it and send it with a sympathy card. A call is appropriate if you choose to make one. In your impact report, put a small asterisk by the deceased person's name and then add a footnote to note that the person is deceased.

Public thank-yous
Letters, notes, and phone calls are the most common formats for thanking donors. These are considered *private* thank-you formats because only donors see them. However, there are other formats that allow you to *publicly* thank donors: radio, television, Internet, publications, naming walls, programming events, and fundraising events.

Always look for ways to publicly thank donors. Why? Donors who are publicly thanked and recognized for their gifts, even small ones, are more likely to give in the future.

You'll need to determine which public formats work best for your non-profit based on available resources, intended purpose, the audience you'd like to reach, and the impact you'd like to make. To get you started, here are some useful tips for three commonly used public thank-you formats.

Annual report or impact report

The most common place to thank and acknowledge donors is in an impact report (annual report). If you publish one of these—and you should—create "Thank You!" categories delineated by the amount of money given. Then, within each category, list the donors who gave at that level in alphabetical order, sorted by last name.

For example, create a "$10,000 or more" category for all donors who gave $10,000 or more, followed by all donors who gave $5,000-$9,999 all the way down to donors who gave $100 or less. Some nonprofits also include an "In-Kind" category. Rainmakers use this display format because they know it brings out donors' competitive spirit and encourages many donors to give at higher levels the following year because they want to be *seen* as giving at a higher level.

Donor walls

A donor wall is a visible way to honor and recognize donor contributions over time. They can include engraved names in brick, raised names made of metal and marble, or names displayed on a giant flat-screen monitor as a virtual donor wall.

If you're going to create some type of public donor wall, don't skimp on the cost. Make it visible, classy, artistic, and appealing. Be sure to have donors sign a document that approves the spelling of their names as you plan to display them. When you unveil the wall, make it a special event and invite the media.

Commemorative naming opportunities

One way to acknowledge and thank major donors is to offer them a chance to name a program, building, playing field, or a room in a school, museum, or art gallery. Rainmakers use this tactic because the ability to commemorate a family name, a loved one, or children can motivate a donor to make a substantial gift. It's also an indelible way to publicly recognize major donors who make large gifts.

Spell the donor's name correctly!

The topic of spelling donors names correctly is so important it's worth mentioning again. Rainmakers want to spell donors names correctly 100 percent of the time because they know misspelling a donor's name just once can result in the loss of a donor.

The larger the donor, the more important it is to ask how they would like their name spelled each time before publishing it. For example, a donor may want his wife's name included with his in your impact report but not in the press release you send out. Also, donors' names change. They marry, separate, divorce, and die. Even the names of foundations and businesses change. Be smart and safe; ask before publishing.

Naming conventions

When publishing a large number of donors, you'll want to devise a naming convention. This is especially important when listing names in an impact report. Traditionally, the man's first name goes with his last name: Karen and John Smith, not John and Karen Smith.

If they have different last names, Kline and Smith respectably, then list the lady's name first: Mrs. Karen Kline and Mr. John Smith. Many donors are less formal nowadays so Karen Kline and John Smith are often acceptable. If you have doubts, err on the side of formality.

Should I send thank-you swag?

Maybe. More and more, donors view thank-you swag such as T-shirts and coffee mugs as a wasteful use of money. If you want to give thank-you gifts to donors, make them meaningful, modest, and connected to your mission. Provide tours of your facility, provide a refrigerator magnet list of the dates of your theater performances, give away a handful of performance tickets, or offer an intimate dinner party with a celebrity.

Cheap and cheesy items like bumper stickers and pens can be an effective swag to thank minor donors, but more and more donors of all sizes see these types of gifts as needless expenses and toss them in the trash. You should also know that donors who *expect* a gift for their donations are more likely to lapse.

"Misspelling a donor's name just once
can result in the loss of a donor."

CHAPTER 30

STEWARDSHIP

As a refresher, cultivation is the process of nurturing relationships with new donors *before* asking them for money, and stewardship is the process of nurturing relationships with existing donors *after* they make a donation. Done well, stewardship transforms donors into loyal, multiyear donors who become dedicated volunteers and enthusiastic mission ambassadors.

Unfortunately, many nonprofits do a terrible job of stewarding donors. They fawn over donors when it's time to ask for money, but have little to no personal contact with them until the next ask: no calls, no meetings, no site tours, no thank-yous, no appreciation dinners . . . just an occasional e-newsletter or piece of direct mail.

Not Rainmakers. They spend the bulk of their fundraising efforts on donor stewardship because they know that a significant portion of a donor's decision to make a future gift is based on how they were treated after making their last gift.

Good stewardship = donor retention = money!
Good stewardship can also help you retain donors. It can take up to two years and a lot of money to secure a gift from a first-time donor, but it may only take a nudge to secure a gift from a current, well-nurtured donor. One of the biggest mistakes nonprofits make is spending money and working tirelessly to acquire donors only to see them slip away due to neglect. Remember, 70-80 percent of first-time donors don't make a second gift, and up to 90 percent stop giving after four years.

Rainmakers don't let this happen. Make a commitment to retain your current donors through exceptional donor stewardship because the more donors you have and the longer they remain loyal, the greater the chances they will increase their giving, contribute in-kind services, provide referrals, and make estate gifts. Now that's good business!

Remember, an ask is little more than a moment in time; stewardship is an ongoing, year-round *process*. Stewardship is where the work is, but it's also where the money is! Use the stewardship tactics outlined on the next page to keep your donors happy and retention rates up.

Exceptional Donor Stewardship:
A 4-Step Process

Rainmakers keep it simple. They follow a stewardship process based on a few general principles and tactics that keep donors informed, engaged, and happy. The process your team develops may be different from the one that follows, but it will get you started if you don't have a process, and if you do have one, it may provide a few new tactics you can add.

1. Nurture the relationship
   a. Yearly guidelines for major donor touches
   b. 7 paths to deeper donor relationships
2. Engage the donor sooner than later
3. Provide meaningful information
4. Do the small stuff

1. Nurture the relationship

People like to do business with people they like and trust. This is why one of the most important goals of the stewardship process is nurturing *personal relationships* with donors. To do this well requires an investment in resources because it takes time, money, and effort to get to know donors, inform them, and engage them, and you need to do all this in a generous and humble manner without annoying them.

A donor's enthusiasm for a mission is typically quite high after making a gift, so a good time to kickoff the nurturing process is during the thank-you process. Your objective is clear: Don't nag, but "touch" your donors regularly to keep them informed and get them involved to deepen their connection with you and the work of your nonprofit. The process is an ongoing one so there is no need to do everything at once.

How many times should you touch a donor per year? This depends on a donor's preference. Too many touches eventually becomes a push. Be patient and take a progressive approach; learn a little more about a donor each time you connect.

When you call or meet with a donor, have a purpose; wasting their time will only irritate them.

Yearly guidelines for major donor touches

1. Face-to-face meetings: 2-3 per year or as desired.

2. Galas and fundraising events: 1-2 or as desired.

3. Small intimate dinners with peers: 1-2 or as desired.

4. Phone calls: Varies. If you think you're calling too much, you most likely are! Calling without a specific reason can annoy donors. Use discretion and make your calls count.

5. Reports and information: Once a quarter or as desired.

6. Social media and email: As desired.

7 paths to deeper donor relationships

1. Increase face-time. Always meet in person when possible.

2. Exceed expectations. Be timely in everything you do. Show up early. Send documents on time. Follow through promptly.

3. Connect with them. Show interest in things that interest them: sports, hobbies, entertainment, technology, current events, etc.

4. Show that you value them. Send unexpected photos. Invite them to exclusive events. Share breaking news with them first. Care for them like you care for your beneficiaries.

5. Be friendly. Be a kind and interesting person they like to see and enjoy talking with. Make them happy and feel good about giving.

6. Take responsibility. Never blame others. Never blame a donor. Be an honest person of impeccable integrity.

7. Personalize everything. Handwrite notes. Thank them in person. Put a personal touch on all correspondence. Think "Concierge Service." Make their experience with you and your nonprofit unexpectedly pleasurable, no matter how small the interaction.

2. Engage the donor sooner than later

Rainmakers know one of the primary reasons donors stop giving is they feel disconnected from the nonprofits they give to. The more you engage donors in the work of your nonprofit, the more emotionally connected they get, and the greater the chance they will become loyal, long-term donors.

One of the key facets of donor stewardship is increasing retention rates by etching a donor's passion for your mission in their head and heart through *experiences* that make them feel connected, fulfilled, and happy.

Below are a number of ideas you can use to engage donors. Some were discussed in the chapter on cultivation. To start the process, design a "donor engagement" form from the list below. Ask donors to use a 1-5 rating scale to rate the strength of their interest for each item. Send out the form each year and work with your staff to create opportunities to engage donors based on the things they expressed interest in.

Ideas for Engaging Donors

1. Become a volunteer
2. Observe programming
3. Meet beneficiaries
4. Tour the facility to meet staff and observe operations
5. Attend outreach and special events
6. Become a community ambassador
7. Speak at special events
8. Join a committee
9. Join the fundraising team
10. Attend a board meeting
11. Become an advisory board member
12. Become a board member
13. Provide a written or video endorsement
14. Provide feedback

Get donors to experience or observe your programming
Nothing will ensure larger and more frequent gifts than getting donors to experience or observe your programming. Firsthand experiences will emotionally glue donors' hearts to the work you do and to those you're helping.

Rainmakers know meaningful donor experiences lead to meaningful gifts. If you can find ways to get your donors to help the hungry kids you're feeding or care for the animals you're sheltering, you won't need to ask them for money—they'll offer.

Conduct more site tours
If a donor hasn't seen your facility, set up a site tour. It provides donors a chance to see your programs, meet your staff, and see the type of facility you work out of. If you're a young nonprofit with a small office and scant furnishings, don't be embarrassed; it's actually a bonus.

The ability to make a substantial impact with modest means impresses donors. Also, make a point to introduce donors to your kindest, hardest-working staff. Most donors are deeply moved by humble souls who are authentically passionate about a mission.

Should you ask major donors to join your board?
That depends. Board membership is a good way to engage major donors, but just because donors are wealthy does not mean they'll make great board members. Many wealthy people like to travel, so they tend to miss a lot of board meetings. Some are extremely busy with their own work and may be reluctant to do board work.

That said, major donors can make terrific board members, but make sure they fit into your culture, add value, and are willing to fulfill their roles and responsibilities. In many cases, major donors make better volunteers, committee members, task force members, advisory board members, and honorary board members.

3. Provide meaningful information
People are busy. Most donors will have an interest in hearing updates from you, but you need to be selective about the types and frequency of information you send them. Since information requirements will vary, it's important you ask. Some donors like social media, some don't. Some prefer email notifications, some prefer text, and some prefer snail mail.

The rule about sending information to donors is simple: ask first. If you annoy donors, they will tune you out and turn off their donation spigots. When you send out your donor engagement form, include a section covering notification preferences. Ask the donor what types of information they would like to receive, how often they would like to receive it, and what formats they prefer.

When you do send information, make it meaningful. Many donors are inundated with contracts and paperwork. They don't have time to read rambling appeal letters and cluttered collateral. So whether you're sending a report, press release, or blog make sure it's courteous, clear, and packs a punch. And when you call, call with a purpose. It's okay to "check in" occasionally, but reserve most calls for important things such as setting up meetings, inviting donors to events, and making thank-you calls. You want to keep donors informed, but you don't want to irritate them. It's a fine line and it's up to you to walk it carefully.

If you can personalize the information you send, so much the better. For example, if you send an impact report, attach a brief note on the cover stating how the donor's gift helped build the facility your kids use everyday. It's small stuff like this that will keep you "top of mind" when donors are thinking of quality nonprofits they like to support.

Donor Portals
Donor portals use cloud technology to keep donors updated and connected. It's similar to the cloud-based customer profile technology your bank and Amazon use. Donors get their own "dashboards" they can log in to so they can check donation history, change contact information, review impact reports, scan calendars for events, sign up to volunteer, receive personalized thank-you notes, choose notification preferences, read blogs, and much more.

Donor portals will revolutionize how nonprofits and donors communicate and connect with each other, and they will improve the efficiency and effectiveness of every stage of the donor lifecycle. Check with the manufacturer of your donor database management system to see if they offer donor portal technology. You may not have the resources to adopt this type of technology now, but it won't be long before it's widespread and affordable.

4. Do the small stuff
You work hard to engage donors and inform them, but sometimes it's the small stuff you do that allows you to stand out from the rest of the fundraisers calling on them. Here are a few Rainmaker favorites.

1. Send a framed picture or poster signed by beneficiaries
2. Take them to lunch with a beneficiary
3. Make them dinner (my favorite!)
4. Honor them at a special event
5. Send a handwritten birthday or anniversary card
6. Send them tickets to a sporting or cultural event

CHAPTER 31

HOSTING EVENTS
THAT RAISE BIG MONEY

Stewardship is the process of touching donors on a regular basis to keep them informed and engaged, and to deepen their connection with you and the work you're doing. The last chapter outlined how you can steward donors through personal interactions and involvement. This chapter outlines how to use specialty events to steward donors and raise money in the process.

Rainmakers like specialty events (gatherings of 10-50 people) because they create a unique stewardship environment that allows donors to see their friends, network with peers, and unite as a group to achieve a common purpose. They also provide a donor experience you cannot duplicate in a one-on-one setting.

If you recall, asking for money in small group settings is the second most effective means of raising money. So hosting specialty events, also known as "boutique" or "salon" events, are not only good places to steward donors, they're good places to raise money. If you're not hosting at least one or two specialty events a year, it's time to start.

The tactics and tips outlined in this chapter will ensure your events are effective, memorable, profitable, and run smoothly.

7 Benefits of Hosting Specialty Events

1. Inform donors of the impact their support is making

2. Collectively unite donors to fulfill your mission

3. Deepen relationships between donors, staff, board, and volunteers

4. Meet prospective donors and recognize existing donors

5. Create networking opportunities for donors

6. Have fun and celebrate with donors, board members, and staff

7. Secure giving commitments and win back lapsed donors

Specialty events provide tremendous value

For a few thousand dollars and a little effort, you can host a classy theme party with sumptuous food and wine. Depending on the number and type of major donors you have, you may be able to raise $50,000, $100,000 or even $250,000! Compared to the enormous amount of time, effort, and money you can spend hosting a full-scale gala to raise the same amount of money, specialty events can be a bargain.

Start the planning process early

No matter what type of event you'd like to host, start the planning process early. You want to make a good impression by hosting a meaningful event and you're not going to be able to do that if you're stressed out, disorganized, and scrambling to work out last-minute details. Budget *twice* as much time as you think it will take.

Start by creating a yearly calendar of the events you'd like to host. Send "save the date" cards to donors at least six months before an event. Assemble a team of event planners willing to organize the events. Develop an event budget and create various checklists of tasks that must be done.

Hosting your first few specialty events will be a little chaotic, but the more you do, the more manageable they become as you create systems and processes for hosting them.

Get people talking about the mission

When hosting a specialty event, have your event team think of fun and engaging ways to get people talking about your mission. A favorite among Rainmakers is to come up with a list of interesting questions for people to answer during dinner.

Pass out the questions halfway through dinner. Break up large tables into groups of 4 or 6. The goal is to have fun, build relationships, and get donors talking about the issues you're facing and the work you do.

After the exercise, you can start the process of raising money, if that's part of the event. If the question exercise was effective, donors should be primed with reasons why it is important to support your mission.

Themes

If you host a specialty event, consider giving it a theme. Events with themes tend to be more memorable and have higher attendance rates, especially if the event is an annual one. If you run a hunger relief organization, host an "Empty Plate" dinner. If you run a museum, host a luncheon based on one of the exhibits you're showing. If you run a land conservation organization, host a wine tasting at one of your nature preserves.

Peer-centric themes are great for local bankers, Rotary members, American Legion members, and realtors. You could also have a sports related theme such as a "Breakfast at Wimbledon" party at a tennis club or a "19th hole cocktail party" at a golf club. If your events are fun and memorable, donors will come back year after year.

7 Ideas for Specialty Events

1. Formal or informal breakfast, lunch, or dinner

2. Wine tasting, celebrity dinner, or art exhibition

3. Theme dinner, event, or holiday party

4. Reception lunch or dinner, or open house

5. A play or musical event with a reception

6. Founder's Day brunch or President's dinner

7. Golf tournament, walkathon, auction, or festival

Call people!
The single best way to get donors to attend a special event is to call them. Let's assume you've sent out invitations and email notices over the last several months. Great. Now, three to seven days before an event you'll want to call each attendee. Remind them of the event, confirm their attendance, and express gratitude for their willingness to attend.

Just before hanging up, leave them with a "hook." Tell them something interesting that will be taking place at the event such as a celebrity that will be performing.

If the couple says they've had a change of plans and cannot attend the event, let them know you'll be contacting them soon to set up a face-to-face meeting to talk about making a gift. They may offer to make a gift on the phone and that's okay, but try to get them to agree to a meeting.

Groom your donors

Rainmakers know that relaxed and happy donors are giving donors. This is why it's important to "groom" donors at events before asking them for money. Here are four ways to get people in the mood for giving big.

1. **Serve great drinks.** Major donors are used to premium wines and spirits. Buy the good stuff. It doesn't cost that much more and it will make a classy impression.

2. **Serve great food.** It's better to serve smaller quantities of higher quality food than having large quantities of low-quality food. The goal is to inspire and entertain people, not feed them. The way to dazzle everyone's palette and create tomorrow's buzz is to serve delicious and slightly unusual food. Always serve a number of dreamy, bite-sized desserts and chocolates.

   If you're serving dinner, do it buffet style, even when serving fancy food. Why? People get to choose the foods they like in the portion sizes they want. If you're the host and like to cook, make a signature dish or dessert. You'll win the hearts of your guests because everyone loves a host who can cook.

3. **Create an inspiring atmosphere**. It's your job to set the tone and vibe of the event. You can do this through music, decorations, the people you choose to speak, and the tactics you use to encourage guests to mingle and get to know one another. The goal is to prepare your guests to write checks. What can you do to create an environment that inspires giving?

4. **Team engagement**. Specialty events provide perfect mingling opportunities. Make sure your team and board members come equipped with specific knowledge of your organization. Provide them with a "Fact Sheet" and your latest impact report a week or two before the event so they can study it and be prepared to talk about your programs, operations, and key financial data.

   Challenge each board member to talk with five donors and thank them for their support. If you have a small number of board members, have the board chair publicly introduce them. It's also a good idea to strategically seat board members near major donors and celebrities during dinner.

Specialty event asks – a 30-minute performance

The wine, dinner, and peer networking at a specialty event always makes for a good time, but you'll need to slice out a segment for the real reason why everyone's attending—to support the mission.

To raise big money at a specialty event, Rainmakers know you must orchestrate the details of the ask process. Every decision will contribute or detract from the success of the event. In fact, your choice to choose one auctioneer over another may mean the difference between raising $20,000 or $200,000.

Below is a basic format for organizing the ask process at a specialty event. Use it as a guideline. Whatever format you use, keep the entire ask portion of the event to 30 minutes. This includes videos, speeches, endorsements, the ask and auctioning process, and time to fill out pledge cards. Once the process exceeds 30 minutes, you'll begin to bore donors and lose donations. Remember, you are hosting a boutique event, not a gala.

7-step Formula for Organizing the Ask Process at a Specialty Event

1. **The welcome** (1-2 minutes). The Board chair, or a celebrity, makes an enthusiastic introduction to welcome guests and thank them for attending. Briefly acknowledge key board members and staff in attendance and mention something about the meaning of the evening and how the next 30 minutes will unfold. Quickly introduce the chief executive.

2. **Chief executive** (2-3 minutes). The chief executive gives a speedy and poignant "State of the organization" talk highlighting the organization's notable accomplishments. These points should center on the impact the organization's work has had on its beneficiaries, the community, and the issues it's addressing. Thank staff and volunteers. Make a connection between the success of the mission and the support of donors.

3. **Endorsements** (1-3 minutes). Have one of your most influential donors, or a celebrity, say a few words about why they support the mission and why they plan on supporting it again this year.

4. **Beneficiary testimonials** (3-5 minutes). Have one or two of your beneficiaries share a story, or show a short video. The stories or video must be powerful, emotional, and compelling. They should show how your work helped them overcome or cope with their challenges. If you use beneficiaries, have them practice their stories many times to reduce stage fright.

5. **The ask** (2-3 minutes). The person doing the ask must be a dynamic and *experienced* public speaker who can make an inspiring ask with confidence and ease. The audience must be moved by the work you're doing and the impact it's having, why you're a good social investment, and why they should support you. It must be sensational!

   This is tall order and crafting such an ask is an art. Do not choose a person for this role based on their title, like a board chair; choose someone who is a great orator and storyteller, someone who loves to speak and knows how to emotionally engage an audience.

6. **The motivator** (10 minutes). Once the ask is made, you'll need someone who can transform the inspiration that's bubbling in the donor's hearts into the motivation of writing checks. The person who made the ask may be the person responsible for doing this, but it is often best to use a professional, like a nonprofit auctioneer.

   The role of the motivator is to get people excited to give. They are masters at reading the room and, on the fly, come up with ways to get donors fired up to dig deeper and give more as they try to achieve the fundraising goals for the evening.

   They facilitate live auction activities, nudge people to match the giving of others, inspire people to pick blocks on a giving pyramid, rally people to achieve a funding goal, keep the atmosphere electric, and discuss the details of filling out pledge cards.

   Rainmakers know that a talented motivator can transform powerful speeches and testimonials into an inspiring and memorable evening of giving. Whenever you can, use a motivator—and choose wisely.

7. Create a moment of silence. This is an optional tactic, but Rainmakers know that it's one of the most effective tactics you can use to increase a donor's level of giving. A moment of silence is effective because it gives donors time to quietly reflect on what they heard and saw, allowing the emotion of the night to sink deeper into their hearts and minds.

The main speaker or the motivator can initiate a moment of silence before they launch into the giving process by saying something like "Let's close our eyes for 30 seconds and use these moments of silence to reflect on the gravity of what we've heard . . . seen . . . and learned . . . and let our hearts decide how we want to support the new children's burn center as we make our commitments."

Quick tip: This tactic also works well at galas and in select face-to-face settings.

A note on galas
In some respects, you can think of galas as large specialty events. If strategically planned and choreographed, they can be effective venues to increase public awareness, build peer-to-peer relationships, acknowledge current donors, cultivate new donors, and fuel support of your mission.

However, Rainmakers know galas are not always the most effective venues to raise money, especially for small nonprofits with limited resources and a small donor base. A gala can cost tens of thousands of dollars and require thousands of hours of labor.

This is fine if a gala brings in hundreds of thousands of dollars. But usually, after factoring in *all* the direct and indirect costs, and *all* the volunteer hours, the net income from a gala is often nominal, sometimes only a few thousand dollars, leaving the event planners feeling deflated.

Plus, planners often overlook the fact that many donors see galas as extravagant wastes while others loathe galas because they get invited to so many of them—"Oh, geez, not another gala!" This can reduce attendance rates and giving amounts.

In most cases, young nonprofits with limited resources and small donor bases will raise more money—sometimes 10 times more—on a dollar-per-hour basis if they redirect an equivalent amount of time, money, and volunteer hours to hosting specialty events and raising money in face-to-face settings.

As your nonprofit grows and your donor pool deepens, you'll want to consider the benefits and weigh the costs of hosting a gala. What is the projected yield? Is it worth it? Would it be more effective to allocate the equivalent amount of resources to other fundraising channels? What can we do to ensure our gala is cost effective and achieves its intended purpose? How can we engage those who attended the gala *after* the gala?

However, if you do decide to host a gala, here are four tactics you should apply to ensure your big event is a big success.

Tips to Make Your Gala a Big Success

1. **Get major donors involved early on.** Secure financial commitments from your biggest donors before the event so you can acknowledge the gifts on the night of the event and leverage them as "lead gifts" to inspire others to give. Also, ask your major donors to support the event by sponsoring tables, speaking at the event, hosting a VIP meet-and-greet, or underwriting event expenses such as catering, speakers, and the auctioneer.

2. **Use an ask formula.** For the ask portion of the gala, follow an ask process similar to the one outlined for specialty events in the previous section. This will ensure your ask is well-orchestrated, giving you the best chance to raise the most amount of money.

3. **Make it memorable**. If you want to raise big money at your gala, you must create an event that people will talk about long after the event is over. What can you do to make the event fun, entertaining, and memorable? Is the theme different and unique? Is the storytelling emotional and moving? The gala must be an event that moves donors so deeply they become inspired to share their experience of the evening with others.

4. **Ask big!** If you're hosting a gala to raise money, then ask big! This is your chance to rally your largest donors and allow them to publicly show their support for your mission. Set lofty fundraising targets. Think creatively about ways you can get people to dig deep and make large sacrificial gifts. Again, secure large lead gifts before the event

and then hire the best auctioneer ever to leverage them on the night of the event.

5. **Invite more wealthy people.** Remember, it takes 200 donors giving $100 each to raise $20,000. If you want to raise big money, you need to invite people who can write big checks—like $5,000 and $20,000 checks. Yes, invite all types of people, but make a special effort to invite people of wealth. Give free tickets to your major donors and encourage them to invite their friends. Over time, your list of major donors will increase and so will the income from your galas.

"If you're not hosting at least one or two specialty events a year, it's time to start."

CHAPTER 32

WHEN THE GIVING ENDS

Adonor's giving is likely to stop at some point. Count on it. Perhaps they moved, found a new nonprofit to support, or had too many bad donor experiences with you. There are many circumstances that influence a donor's decision to stop giving; some you can control, some you cannot.

Whatever the reason or circumstance, when a donor stops giving, or gives an indication they may stop giving (e.g., stops volunteering or stops attending specialty events), Rainmakers take swift action. They want to know what's going on and then determine a course of action to help resolve any issues, or create a smooth and gracious exit.

This chapter will help you recognize some of the circumstances and reasons that cause donors to stop giving so you make an effort to prevent them from happening. It also provides tactics on how to keep donors happy once they decide to stop giving.

8 Reasons Why Donors Stop Giving

1. **Feeling unappreciated.** The most common reasons why donors stop giving is that they feel unappreciated, undervalued, neglected, or the nonprofit they gave to failed to thank them.

2. **Underperformance.** Donors want to make a difference. If they feel their money is not making a difference, or that the nonprofit is underperforming, they leave.

3. **Annoyance.** Donors get turned off if they receive too many appeals, too many phone calls, feel used, or they are uninformed about how the nonprofit used their donation. More than 60 percent of nonprofits call donors only to ask for money.

4. **Terrible service.** Failing to keep a donor informed, responding slowly to requests, failing to follow through, and treating a donor rudely can slam shut a donor's checkbook. A service-driven culture will always raise more money than a money-driven culture.

5. **Unforeseen circumstances.** A donor may unexpectedly become divorced, widowed, or jobless. A donor may become preoccupied with cancer therapy, an ailing parent, an extended vacation, or get hit with a surprise expense such as a tuition bill, tax liability, or home repair. When personal and financial burdens take a front seat, donations often take a back seat.

6. **Drama and controversy.** If donors get wind about board drama, a scandal, embezzled funds, or squandered resources, they often run for the hills.

7. **Changes in philanthropic objectives.** Some donors like to fund a nonprofit for two or three years and then move on to another nonprofit. It's not that they don't like you or your mission, it's just that their interests change—and that's okay.

8. **For-profit motives.** Some donors need to adjust their financial portfolios to start a business, make an investment, or reduce a debt. These changes can force donors to suspend or stop their giving.

When giving stops, make contact and do something nice
As soon as a major donor misses a pledge payment, or fails to renew an annual gift, it's time to make contact. For minor donors, make a call unless you have thousands of them and not enough staff to make calls. In this case, contact donors using email or regular mail.

For major donors, try to set up a face-to-face meeting. This may not be possible if the donor lives out of state, or it may not be preferable based on the situation. When you call, no matter what size donor you're contacting, be polite and grateful, and tactfully ask the donor what brought about the change. If there is something you can say or do to resolve the issue, do it.

Otherwise, if the donor clearly wants to end their support—for whatever reason—acknowledge their decision and graciously thank them. If you're talking with a major donor on the phone, tell them you'd like to take them out for coffee or lunch to thank them in person.

You may also want to formally acknowledge them with a plaque, engrave their name on a wall, or write a story about them in your impact report or quarterly newsletter. Another nice touch is to have one of your beneficiaries send a photo and write a note of appreciation, and have one of your board members call them.

Even when donors stop giving, they may still want to be connected to you. Ask them if they want to remain on your email and social media lists, receive your impact report, and be invited to events.

Keep your brand shiny

It's imperative that a donor's exit be amicable, gracious, and memorable because donors talk. Never alienate or shun a donor when they stop giving, and never say anything bad or gossip about a donor. If you do, it's sure to leak into the donor community and rebound to hurt your brand and funding, possibly for years. Remind staff and board members on a regular basis to make only positive, benevolent comments about former donors, no matter how unruly and difficult they were.

Combat lapsed donors and donor attrition

Some nonprofits make the egregious error of waiting a year, sometimes two, to call a lapsed donor. When they finally call, they give a lame excuse why they neglected the donor. This usually reinforces the reasons why the donor stopped giving.

If you have lapsed donors, you should definitely try to reengage them by writing, calling, or meeting with them. But don't wait too long because with each passing month the chances of them reinstating shrinks.

Rainmakers know the best way to combat lapsed donors is to keep close tabs on donor giving patterns. Have the person responsible for your donor database set time thresholds for different types of donors. Once a donor's giving lapses beyond a threshold, a team member can launch an action plan to address the situation.

The good news is, if you contact lapsed donors quickly enough by calling or meeting them, reactivation can be as high as 60 percent.

Donor attrition is inevitable so it's important to develop a year-round strategy to find and cultivate new donors. Why? Because having more donors, especially major donors, increases your chances of raising additional funds. It also reduces "funding risk" because a larger percentage of your income will be spread out over a greater number of donors.

More importantly, you'll want to have a detailed strategy for retaining current donors because the longer your donors remain loyal, the more money and benefits you stand to receive.

Always remember, existing donors are the most cost-effective source of additional income. A new donor can cost five times more to acquire than a lapsed donor costs to reactivate, and it can cost up to 10 times more to acquire a new donor than to keep in touch with an existing one. Plus, a mere 10 percent reduction in donor attrition can lead to a 100 percent increase in lifetime value of all your donors over 10 years.

Donor retention is lucrative. Donor churn is costly. It will cost you time, money, and opportunity. The way to combat churn is to make an *ongoing* effort to steward existing donors in a manner that makes them feel valued, appreciated, and inspired, and to get them involved in the work of your nonprofit.

"If there is no relationship between
the asker and donor, and the donor is ignored,
you will lose the donor. Period."

CHAPTER 33

FOUNDATION, CORPORATE, AND GOVERNMENT GIVING

Roughly five percent of all non-government, charitable giving comes from corporations; 15 percent comes from foundations; and 80 percent comes from individuals. The government is also a gracious funder, but of the $137 billion it gives, the lion's share goes to education, health care, and large cultural organizations.

Gifts from corporations, foundations, and government agencies are vital to the nonprofit world. Many make large, multiyear commitments, and for some nonprofits, these sources of funding are their *only* sources of funding.

When it comes to philanthropy, foundations, corporations, and government agencies share many of the same goals as donors: They are Super 6 seekers! They like to support issues they care about, missions they believe in, organizations they trust, people they like, first-rate performance and impact, and outstanding customer service and donor relations. For more on Super 6 attributes, see Chapter 6.

What follows is a set of tactics you can use to secure gifts from these funders and stay in good favor with them after you receive funding.

First, weigh the costs!
Securing funding from any source is typically a welcomed gift. However, many nonprofits are short on resources and the staggering amount of time they spend to secure and maintain grants can greatly reduce the time they spend on raising money from individuals, which in some cases, can mean a loss of income.

A grant application may take dozens of hours to complete. Waiting for approval may take months. Waiting for a check may take many more months. When the check arrives, the amount funded may be much less than expected and the reporting requirements may require more work than expected. Plus, some organizations have limits on how much they can give you based on your budget size.

On the other hand, some grants are headache-free and easy to get. The application process may be nothing more than a two-page online questionnaire, the approval process is quick, checks arrive quickly, and the reporting process is minimal.

So, are grants (and sponsorships) worth the time and effort? Maybe. As a Rainmaker, it's your job to assess the costs and benefits of each opportunity. Ask questions: Is this funding opportunity worth the time and resources we're going to have to put forth? Or, would it be better to spend the same amount of time and resources on cultivating donors, hosting specialty events, and raising money in face-to-face settings?

Is it better to secure a grant that might last only two years, or secure more donors who might become loyal givers for five, 10, or 20 years? How can you invest your capacity in a way that will provide the best *long-term* results? There's a healthy balance and it's your responsibility to adjust the scales based on resources, expertise, and funding goals.

Corporate Giving

Types of corporate gifts

1. **Sponsorships.** Corporations and businesses of all sizes like sponsorships because they're great PR and allow them to show people how much they care about their communities. They give money and in-kind services, and in return get their name prominently displayed at events, in marketing material, and in the media. They might also get a few perks such as free tickets, VIP access, and drink coupons.

2. **In-kind gifts.** More and more companies are willing to support nonprofits by getting their staff involved as volunteers rather than writing checks. This is a bonus to nonprofits because more volunteers mean more human capital and the possibility of more donors. Plus, if a company's staff has a great experience volunteering with you, it increases the likelihood that the company will make a cash donation.

   Many in-kind corporate contributions can provide significant value to nonprofits. Accounting firms can provide bookkeeping and accounting services, law offices can provide legal advice, and marketing companies can provide graphic design services. However, companies don't know how they can help unless you call on them. Pick up the phone, express your needs, and find ways to get the company's staff involved.

3. **Cash and grants.** Most companies, regardless of size, have charitable giving budgets. When seeking cash donations, local and regional businesses are your best targets because they tend to support local nonprofits whose services benefit the community.

Don't expect large companies to make large gifts. Donation sizes can vary. Some Fortune 500 companies make small grants that require detailed applications and reporting, while some small businesses make large gifts that require no application or reporting. Determine if the size of the gift is worth the effort to secure it.

4. **Employee matching.** Matching gift programs are charitable giving programs set up by a company in which the company matches donations made to a nonprofit by its employees. Companies typically match on a 1:1 basis, but sometimes they match at ratios of 2:1 or 3:1.

Matching gift programs can be very effective, especially after you've engaged a set of employees as volunteers. If they have a meaningful volunteer experience, they may be willing to "champion" the matching gift program to coworkers who did not volunteer.

5. **Cause marketing.** There are many variations of this type of giving program, but the most common type is when a company commits to giving a percentage of its sales of certain products or services to a selected nonprofit.

The problem? The amount of money received is typically small unless you have an agreement with a large company willing to give you a large percentage of sales proceeds.

Before you agree to a cause marketing deal, conduct a detailed cost benefit analysis to determine if it's worth the time and resources you'll have to put into it.

Quick tip: Cause marketing is more effective among Millennials than Baby Boomers.

Tactics to win corporate gifts

1. **Do your homework first.** Before you send a proposal, find out some information about the company's philanthropic profile. What issues are important to them? Is there a good fit between what you do and what they fund? What types of nonprofits have they funded? Do they prefer sponsorships or grants? What size gifts do they make? Do they have an employee volunteer program? Do they have an employee donation-matching program?

2. **Target local companies first.** Target local companies first because they like to support local nonprofits. After that, you can expand your reach by geographic regions. One of the biggest advantages of working with local businesses is that the owners are typically more accessible, more involved, more flexible, cut checks more quickly, and require less paperwork.

3. **Get a meeting with a decision maker.** Climbing your way up the corporate decision-making ladder can be exhausting. Find out who the decision makers are and talk with your team and board members to find out how they can help you set up a meeting. If you get a meeting, try to hold it at a location where your programming is taking place to increase your chances of getting a "Yes" to your ask.

4. **Help improve a company's image in the community.** Corporate philanthropy and corporate image go hand in hand. It's critical you show companies how you plan to recognize them and their gifts. Show them how you plan to highlight them in social media, on your website, on television and radio, at an event, and in promotional material. You may even be able to demonstrate how their involvement will improve staff morale and increase sales.

5. **Show impact.** Companies are keenly aware of ROI (return on investment). If you want to win corporate funds, show them the success of your work in terms of ROSI (return on social investment). Show them the impact their gifts will have on your beneficiaries, the community, employees, customers, the issues you're addressing, and their community image and corporate objectives.

6. **Target the marketing department.** Most corporate sponsorships are funded through a company's marketing department. This typically means less hassle and faster turnaround times. Therefore, if you're

looking for a large company to underwrite the catering expenses of your gala, call the marketing department, not their foundation.

7. **Start with volunteers.** If you want to get companies to fund your mission, get their employees involved first. Offer non-programming opportunities as well as programming opportunities. Ask for in-kind gifts such as Web design work, strategic planning guidance, investment oversight, and brand management.

   If you're hosting a programming event or fundraising event, get corporate teams to pitch in. As more volunteers have meaningful moments with your nonprofit, more executives will notice, which will lead to greater levels of funding. You may also want to ask a volunteer or an executive to join your advisory board.

Foundation Giving

Tactics to win foundation grants

1. **Do your homework first.** Learn about a foundation's philanthropic profile before submitting a grant. What issues are important to them? What types of nonprofits have they funded? Is there a good fit between what you do and what they fund? What are their giving guidelines? What are their reporting requirements? What size gifts do they make? Is the grant amount worth the time and effort you'll need to put forth to secure it?

2. **Start small.** Small, local foundations are good targets because they like to fund nonprofits that are making a difference in the communities in which they operate. Applications can be as short as one page and reporting requirements are typically nominal.

   After securing a handful of local grants, move on to regional and national foundations. They will be more open to funding you once they see you have the ability to secure local grants from small and medium-sized foundations.

3. **Show impact.** Foundations are all about performance and impact. You must demonstrate the work you're doing is making a meaningful impact on the people you serve, the community, society, the environment, the issue you're addressing, or whatever. It needs to be clear and it needs to be measurable, and you should present it in a

powerful and compelling manner. Keep in mind, it's more impressive to show how *deep* you are than how big you are, or how fast you're growing.

4. **Meet with them.** Foundations don't make decisions, people do. If you can arrange a visit at a foundation to meet a grants manager or a trustee, make it happen. Better yet, set up a visit so they can meet your team, see your facility, and observe your programming.

Once you get funded, it's important to nurture your relationships with grants managers and trustees because if they like *you,* and your nonprofit is making big-time impact, you'll find yourself in good favor to secure future grants.

5. **Write a standout grant.** Many foundations see hundreds, sometimes thousands, of grant applications a year. Most nonprofits write shoddy grants. To get funded consistently, your grants need to be professional grade, not "Let's just get it done" grade. Be cautious about using interns and inexperienced grant writers. You may lose precious grant funding due to careless and substandard writing skills.

Follow grant guidelines carefully. The writing should be typo free and grammatically correct. The layout and design should be clean and sharp. The content should be concise and compelling. The graphics must pop. If you spend the time to write a few standout grants, you can leverage the hard work because a lot of the information is transferable to other grant applications.

6. **Ask for modest funding first.** A surefire way to have your grant tossed in the trash is to ask for an exceptionally large first-time grant, say $100,000, when a foundation's first-time grants range between $10,000 and $20,000.

For a first-time grant, it's wise to exhibit modesty and ask for an amount at the middle or lower end of a foundation's first-time grant range. It's more important to get funded than to ask big and risk not being funded. Why? Because once you get funded and you prove your worth, you'll have opportunities to ask for much larger amounts of money.

Government Giving

Tactics to win government grants

1. **Community support.** Government agencies are leery of funding new and unproven nonprofits. If you can show your programs and organization have widespread community support, agencies will look at you more favorably.

2. **Start locally.** When you first apply for government funding, try to secure a small grant from a local or regional agency. If you're successful at this level, federal grants will be easier to secure. Plus, you'll learn a lot about how the government grant-making process works. This is an important strategy because it's better to make mistakes on small grants than to lose a large grant due to inexperience.

3. **History of successful performance and impact.** Government agencies are big on track records. They want to see three to five years of consistent high-performance and specific outcomes and impact. You want to show agencies as many measurable results as possible because the more you have, and the more persuasive they are, the better your chances of getting funded.

4. **Best practices.** The government is a big fan of best practices. They tend to be cautious about "new" and "different" but embrace "innovative" and "improvement." Whenever you can, show that you are following, plan to follow, or plan to create industry best practices.

5. **Evaluation plan.** If you want to impress government agencies, show them you have an evaluation process in place for your programs and operations. Your evaluation methodologies don't have to be complicated, just thorough enough to show that you're concerned about efficiency, effectiveness, performance, and accountability.

6. **Model organization.** Government agencies like to support model programs. If you can show that your programs, services, or methods of operation can be a model for other nonprofits, a sector, or for an issue, agencies will look at you favorably. If what you do can also be easily scaled, leveraged, or replicated, that's even better.

CHAPTER 34

MARKETING QUIVER CHECKLIST

R ainmakers build a quiver of high quality marketing collateral to equip themselves and their team members with the information they need to educate, inspire, and motivate themselves as well as donors. You may not have the resources to build all of the following "arrows" at once, but build the ones you can and make a commitment to build the others as resources permit.

Whatever you do, don't skimp. Impressions do make a difference so spend the money to create professional, eye-popping, attention-grabbing material that's clear, concise, creative, educational, inspiring, motivating, and entertaining. Yes, that's a tall order, but Rainmakers know attention to detail and making memorable impressions can transform passive donors into passionate donors.

Marketing Quiver Checklist

1. Impact report

2. Your story

3. Website

4. 30-second organizational overview

5. Mission, vision, and culture statements

6. Fact sheet

7. Giving props

8. Program descriptions

9. PowerPoint presentation

10. Financials

11. Short promotional video

12. Testimonials, endorsements, and personal stories

13. Correspondence and proposal templates

14. Bios of board members and key staff

15. Annual IRS 990s and IRS 501(c)3 Determination Letter

1. Impact report (annual report)

No marketing document is more important than your impact report. If done well, it's an entire marketing quiver wrapped into one document. If done amazingly well, donors will actually read it and be compelled to act in some way. If done poorly, people will skim the captions, smile at a picture or two, and then use it for kindling.

To find good examples, seek out 20 exemplary organizations and ask them to send their impact reports. If you have limited funds for graphic design work, make sure you allocate a good portion of it for this document. Fill the report with powerful testimonials, high quality emotional photos, and compelling copy.

If you're a startup, you should still develop a document like an impact report that contains much of the same material. You just need to spin the copy and talk about the present and future, not the past. Talk about the money you plan to raise, the programs you plan to build, and impact you plan to make. Call it a Launch Report or Business Report.

2. Your story (case for support)

The goal here is to create a brief narrative (two or three pages) that team members can use to tell donors who you are, what you do, why you do it, how you do what you do, who you have done it for, what makes you different, what impact it's had, and why it's worthy of support. It can also provide details of projects you want donors to support including costs, revenue projections, milestones, and plans for sustainability.

Your story is a key arrow in your marketing quiver because it serves many functions. Once developed, it becomes a resource for the creation of other material such as grant proposals, fundraising brochures, and copy for speeches, presentations, and promotional collateral.

It can also help ensure that the board and staff are delivering consistent messages about your nonprofit. If you need help developing your story or case for support, search the web; you'll find plenty of books and sample templates.

3. Website

Donors will visit your website—bank on it! And it will make an impression, which is why your site needs to be amazing. The site should be clean, up-to-date, easy to navigate, informative, entertaining, and inspiring. Use plenty of white space, videos, stories, testimonials, and photos. Make it easy for readers to learn about who you are, what you do, the impact you're making, and how they can get involved.

Keep your homepage simple. Use lots of photos and graphics and go light on text. Have a button or graphic that allows people to donate. Find a talented website developer to design a dazzling site with distinct messaging that motivates visitors to come back.

4. 30-second organizational overview

This is a *must* have. Develop a short, 30-second overview of who you are, what you do, why you do it (value, relevance), the impact you're having, and why it's cool to be involved.

This is NOT an "elevator pitch." You are not pitching (selling) anything. The purpose of this content is to help you share basic information about your nonprofit with people who might not know anything about it. Think of your overview as a series of sound bites to start a dialogue about your nonprofit with the intention of drawing listeners into more thoughtful conversation.

It's best to create a 30-second overview template that team members agree on and then let members modify the template to their liking so their version of the overview will be unique to them.

5. Mission, vision, and culture statements

These statements are the backbone of what you do, why you exist, what you aspire to accomplish, and what you believe. If you need help building these statements, you'll find many resources on the Web.

The essence and driving force behind these statements should be in the forefront of your mind every time you speak to a donor. Everyone on your fundraising team should be able to clearly articulate these statements, if only in their own words. Write them in your impact report and occasionally write one of them in the marketing material you're sharing with donors.

6. Fact sheet

A fact sheet highlights the most impressive facts and accomplishments of your nonprofit. Keep it to one page. Focus on information that will impress and wow donors.

This document is also a great training tool for your fundraising team. They can refer to it directly or memorize key facts. "We served 2,000 meals to homeless children last year . . . a 50 percent increase over last year." "We've reduced the percentage of money that we use for fund-raising from 20 percent to 10 percent." "Enrollment in our high school literacy program jumped 27 percent in the last six months."

7. Giving props
Competitive giving environments can motivate donors to give. When they know they are part of a collective (community) effort, their competitive spirit springs into action to dig deep to help reach a goal.

Fundraising props come in many varieties such as gift tables, giving clubs, matching gifts, pyramid gifts, lead gifts, sponsorship lists, and wish lists. You want to create a variety of props because they will help your team raise more money by making the process of asking for money easier for them and for donors (For examples, see Chapter 23).

Once you create a prop, you simply present it to a donor when asking for money. The ask is spelled out because the choices are displayed visually. A donor need only choose—based on a little prompting from the asker—how they would like to participate. This takes pressure off the asker since the prop provides the ask, and it takes pressure off a donor because it provides them with a list of choices.

8. Program descriptions
"Tell me about your programs" is one of the most common inquiries you'll hear from donors. At a minimum, you should develop a document that gives an overview of each program and service you offer. You can then create variations to use in your impact report and on your website.

The descriptions you write should be brief, no longer than two or three paragraphs. Most nonprofits spend too much time writing about how their programs function. That's not what donors want to hear. They care about what your programs accomplish and the impact they're having on people, families, your community, the environment, the sector you work in, and the issues you're addressing.

Your goal should be to write compelling copy that captures attention and shows impact. Less is better. If donors want to know more about the nuts and bolts of how things run, they'll ask.

9. PowerPoint presentation

To raise money, you need to do lots of show-and-tell. A short Power-Point presentation is an effective tool for showing donors why your nonprofit is worthy of support. When done right, the presentation becomes a visual representation of key information and images you want people to know and see.

You can use the PowerPoint as a presentation prop when meeting with donors in face-to-face settings, or in large group settings such as cultivation events and specialty fundraising events. You can also use them when speaking to community service organizations, foundation trustees, or corporate executives.

Whatever the use, the PowerPoint should be short. Target 15 minutes or less with 20 or fewer slides. To be effective, go light on text and heavy on impact. Use generous amounts of high quality photos, graphic elements, and whitespace. Focus most of the content on the impact your work is having—not what you do. Supplement the slides with powerful stories and testimonials, a little history, your vision, how people can get involved and, if you're asking for money, how people can give.

When sent with a compelling video, a well-crafted PowerPoint can be a powerful tool to share with donors and foundations *before* you meet with them so they get a quick glance into what you do. It can also act as a teaching aid to help your team and volunteers refine their knowledge about your nonprofit. The more comfortable people are talking about the work and impact of your nonprofit, the more money they'll raise.

10. Financials

Many major donors and nearly every foundation, corporation, and government agency will ask to see your financial statements before making a donation. The three most requested documents are: statement of activities (income statement), statement of financial position (balance sheet), and an annual budget.

Most nonprofits produce shoddy looking financial statements. After crunching the numbers, spend a little time to make your statements shine. Create graphs, pie charts, and infographics. Use highlights and color to make the important figures stand out. Impressions matter. If your financials look professional, you'll look professional, and the likelihood of getting funded will increase.

11. Short promotional video

Videos have massive power to motivate donors. You must create at least one spectacular video that inspires people to get involved and take action. To produce a jaw-dropping video, use a professional videographer. Amateurs tend to produce bland videos that "tell" people information, but lack the sizzle and emotion that "move" people.

For the length of your videos, target three to four minutes. Tell touching stories that show the impact you're making. If you have the funds, it's also good to build a few 30 to 60-second video clips that you can post on your website. These can be fun, entertaining, amateur videos that showcase program activities, client testimonials, or donor endorsements.

12. Testimonials, endorsements, and personal stories

Few things lend more credibility to a worthy mission than a powerful testimonial endorsing your nonprofit and the work it's doing. A single endorsement may be all a donor needs to write a big check.

Develop a process to collect written and video testimonials and endorsements. Beneficiary testimonials are best, followed by donor and celebrity endorsements. Also, try to get testimonials and endorsements from people of authority or stature in your community.

Testimonials and endorsements are no good unless you use them. Include them in letters you send donors. Show donors a list of endorsements when asking them for money. Sprinkle them liberally on your website, in videos, in your impact report, and in promotional material. You can also have people present their testimonials and endorsements during radio or television interviews, during fundraising events, or when speaking to community service organizations.

13. Correspondence and proposal templates

If a major donor receives six different documents from your nonprofit and each has its own font style and format, it screams "unprofessional." Have a graphic artist create a set of layout and design standards (style guide) for your nonprofit. This way, team members will know what font and layout to use when crafting letters, emails, and marketing collateral.

Once you have a style guide in place, create templates for documents you use regularly: thank-you letters, acknowledgement letters, and proposals. This way, all your correspondence will have the same look and feel, creating unity and a professional image.

Another good idea is to create a secure area of your website where your team and board members can download versions of your letterhead and template documents so they can use them to create documents they share with donors.

14. Bios of board members and key staff

Many donors have strong business backgrounds. They know great organizations have great people running them. A set of high quality board and staff bios can generate enormous credibility. In fact, a set of bios may be all the assurance a donor needs to feel their donation will be used wisely.

Create printable and website versions of your bios. Keep them brief, one to two *short* paragraphs. The trend is 100 words or less. Include a high quality photo. The photos can be fun or professional, but whatever style you choose, they should be consistent and shot by a professional.

Bios with a line or two of humor in them can add personality to the bios and your nonprofit. "When Tim isn't running his software company, you'll find him enjoying his favorite hobby . . . feeding great white sharks off the coast of Monterey Bay."

15. Annual IRS 990s and IRS 501(c)3 Determination Letter

The IRS requires nonprofits to complete an IRS 990 tax form each year. It's a long and somewhat cumbersome document to produce. However, the majority of foundations, corporations, and your largest donors will want to review your 990s to see how well you're managing your nonprofit and the money you raise.

The IRS 501(c)3 Determination Letter is a letter the IRS sends to nonprofits to notify them that they have received tax-exempt status. Most of your biggest donors will request a copy of this document to assure them that you were legally granted 501(c)3 tax-exempt status.

You'll get asked for these two documents a lot. Convert them to PDF format and place them on your website for easy viewing, downloading, and sharing. You'll also want to print a few hardcopies to have on hand for distribution.

CHAPTER 35

13 WAYS TO ENSURE FUNDRAISING FAILURE

1. Require, force, or coerce people to raise money who are fearful of it, loathe it, or resent having to do it.

2. Hire a chief executive who dislikes fundraising, or keep a chief executive who isn't good at fundraising and is unwilling to improve their skills.

3. Allow inexperienced people to make key decisions about fundraising strategies, events, and messaging.

4. Fail to support and appreciate your fundraising team.

5. Spend too much time writing small grants and hosting low-yield fundraisers relative to the time you spend meeting donors in face-to-face settings and hosting specialty events.

6. Spend too much time and money trying to find new donors and too little time and money stewarding current donors.

7. Spend too little time cultivating donors before asking for first-time donations.

8. Don't create a fundraising plan, or a committed team to execute it, or the infrastructure necessary to support it.

9. Allow board members to neglect their fundraising responsibilities, including making a donation.

10. Set unrealistic fundraising goals and expectations.

11. Assign your fundraising team non-fundraising tasks.

12. Ignore the significance of high quality marketing as it relates to fundraising success.

13. View fundraising expenses, including expenses for staff, as a waste of money instead of wise investments.

CHAPTER 36

15 THINGS THAT
ANNOY DONORS

1. Treating them like cash machines.

2. Poor customer service.

3. Acting too eager and pushy to get a donation.

4. Neglecting to build—and nurture—a relationship with them.

5. Not thanking them after they've made a donation.

6. Listening too little and talking too much, especially about yourself or your organization.

7. Not showing them how their money is making a difference.

8. Not caring about their personal interests, hobbies, philanthropic goals, and family.

9. Excessive emails, calls, letters, and meetings.

10. Being fake, sucking up, and fawning over them.

11. Not understanding basic information about your organization.

12. Expressing too little gratitude and appreciation for the non-monetary gifts they make.

13. Disorganization, unprofessionalism, and not following through.

14. Canned solicitation pitches and form letters.

15. Failure to offer a choice in the types, frequency, and delivery methods of communications they receive.

CHAPTER 37

12 TIPS FOR OVERCOMING FEARS AND ANXIETIES

Are you nervous about asking donors for money? If you answered "Yes" you're in good company because these feelings are common, even among Rainmakers. Some people fear rejection and failing. Some feel uneasy when meeting people of wealth, and others worry about offending friends.

If you're truly terrified of asking people for money, or you hate it, loathe it, or would rather have your mouth washed out with soap, then don't do it! No one should *ever* be forced—or feel forced—to ask for money because it may result in a bad donor experience, loss of a donation, loss of a donor, or loss of the person asking for money.

Now, if you're a little fearful of fundraising but have a positive attitude and a desire to learn, then there are a number of things you can do to overcome many of the fears and anxieties you may have about raising money. Listed below are some tactics you can adopt to turn fear and anxiety into strength and courage.

1. **I'm not good at asking for money.** No one is when they first start. It's like any skill; you improve by learning and practicing. Make a commitment to learn, practice, and apply the principles and tactics in this book, and from other books and resources, and work with a member of your team who is willing to coach or mentor you.

    Practice on your team members and family members first. Next, ask new and current donors for non-monetary gifts such as favors and in-kind services, or invite them to events or site tours. This is a good way to gain experience and learn from your mistakes without the risk of losing funding. When you start asking for money, start with minor donors and work your way up from there. It's a lot easier asking for $200 than $20,000.

2. **I'm not good at glad-handing or kissing up.** That's good, neither are Rainmakers. Donors loathe "sales" types. Reframe the context. You are not glad-handing, you're sharing your passion and encouraging people to support your worthy mission.

3. **You feel your organization isn't worthy of support.** If this is the case, decline from asking people for money. You must believe in your nonprofit, even if it's struggling. If you don't, you'll be self-conscious and your passion will appear fake. When donors notice this, they'll close their checkbooks.

4. **What if I forget what to say or freeze up?** You'll have frozen moments, and they can be nerve-wracking, but you'll get through them without getting frostbite. The more you learn and practice, the fewer freeze ups you'll have. This is also why it's wise to start out by talking with small donors and asking for non-monetary gifts and favors.

5. **I don't know the person well enough.** This is common, which is why it's important to get to know donors in casual settings such as cultivation events and in-person meetings *before* you ask them for money. It's also a good strategy to have someone who knows you and the donor make an introduction.

6. **I'm not sure the person has much money to donate.** Ask around. Perhaps a board member or volunteer knows the donor's giving patterns and net worth. If you've done a good job cultivating the donor, you should have some idea. However, if you don't, ask for a modest gift. The worst that can happen is that the donor will say the amount is too high.

7. **The donor already supports a cause like ours, why would they support us?** Perhaps the donor cares deeply about a particular issue like poverty and is willing to support more than one nonprofit that addresses the issue. Tell the donor how your nonprofit differentiates itself and how it complements the work of other nonprofits addressing the issue of poverty.

   Also, ask the donor to pledge a small donation to "test drive" your nonprofit so you can prove to them that the impact you're making is a good social investment. If you dazzle them with outstanding donor relations and high-performance impact, you're likely to get a much larger donation the next time you ask.

8. **If I ask her for money, she is going to ask me for money.** Keep the focus on your nonprofit, not your friendship. You want to get your friend emotionally connected to your mission before asking her to donate so she contributes based on a *desire* to give, not an *obligation* to give, especially if you hope she will become a longtime donor.

Another tactic is not to make the ask. Instead, cultivate the relationship and be an advocate of the mission, but have someone else do the asking. If the donor does ask you to donate to her pet nonprofit, let her know that you *may* donate based on your passion in the mission, but she should not *expect* that you will donate. It's often a good idea to disclose a statement like this to donors before you ask them for money.

9. **I can't possibly ask a friend, relative, or colleague for money.** Then don't. Again, be a cultivator of the relationship and a champion of the mission, and then have someone else make the ask.

10. **What if the donor says "No" and never speaks to me again?** You may think this, but it's extremely unlikely—especially if you've properly cultivated the donor and ask for a donation in a respectful and humble manner. Donors are generally kind and understanding; they know you're doing a job or fulfilling a responsibility.

11. **I'm afraid they are going to ask me something I don't know.** They might. It happens. This is why you want to learn as much as you can about your nonprofit. However, if a donor does ask a question you can't answer, be honest. Tell them that you don't know the answer and that you'll find out (most likely from the chief executive) and get back to them within 24 hours.

12. **The economy is tough right now; it's tacky to ask.** It's not tacky to ask. It's tacky if you ask in a tactless manner. During tough economic times, some donors feel a pinch and some don't. Your job is to make a good case why your program needs support during tough times. Be sensitive to changes in a donor's financial position and offer a pledge opportunity where they can pay their gift over an extended period of time, possibly with the option of deferring the first payment for a few months.

> "No one is good when they first
> start asking for money. It's like any skill;
> you improve by learning and practicing."

CHAPTER 38

KEY DATA TO COLLECT FROM DONORS

The more you know about your donors, the greater the likelihood they will remain loyal, gracious donors. What follows is a list of donor information Rainmakers like to track. There is no need to collect all the information at once. Start with "The Basics" and then slowly gather more information from your donors each time you connect with them.

It's futile trying to remember all the information you learn. Therefore, set up a process where your team can enter "donor profile" information directly into your donor database system. Cloud based systems are best. They allow you to store information in a secure but accessible format so team members can quickly update and access profile information to manage donors and prepare for meetings.

Now, the day will come when your chief executive will leave your nonprofit—perhaps on good terms, perhaps not. If you don't have a process and policies in place for storing donor information, then all the donor information they acquired from all donors they managed will walk out the door when they leave. Not good.

This holds true for anyone who manages donors. If a number of people leave at once, it can be devastating to a fundraising program and greatly hamper a nonprofit's ability to raise money and retain donors. Be wise. Create a system to safely store and share donor profile information.

Key Data to Collect from Donors

1. **The basics.** Address, email, phone numbers (mobile is key), birthday, education, names of family members, website, and most used social media sites.

2. **Fun stuff.** Favorite hobbies, interests, clubs, recreational activities, and favorite types of music, movies, and television shows.

3. **Motivation.** Why is the donor passionate about your mission? Why does the donor like your nonprofit? What are the donor's philanthropic goals and interests?

4. **Appeal strategies.** What are the best fundraising strategies and tactics to use when asking this donor for money? For example, "The donor always likes to meet at their home in the afternoons and they do not like to attend large galas."

5. **Giving history.** How much has the donor given? How many times has the donor given? What is the donor's average gift size? When does the donor like to give? Does the donor have a pet program?

6. **Event Attendance.** What events has the donor attended? What were the dates? Did the donor participate in any significant way? What style of event does the donor like to attend?

7. **Affiliations.** Does the donor belong to any professional associations or clubs? What about board appointments or volunteer work at other nonprofits? What's the donor's work history?

8. **Significant achievements.** Ask the donor to highlight anything of importance such as military service, public service, books authored, awards, honors, inventions, and life achievements.

9. **Internal connections.** Does the donor have a relationship with any staff member, board member, volunteer, or beneficiary of your organization? What is the relationship?

10. **Correspondence history.** What proposals, letters, and significant collateral have you sent? What type of collateral do they prefer? How do they like to be contacted: phone, email, text? How frequently do they like to be contacted?

"Require donor profiles.
Board and staff will leave your nonprofit.
When they do, you don't want your
corporate intelligence to leave with them."

CHAPTER 39

5-STEP RAINMAKER TRAINING REGIMEN

Rainmakers are good at fundraising because they spend time learning and practicing the craft. Encourage your team to adopt the following training regimen and practice on each other to build confidence and keep their fundraising muscles toned as they progress to more advanced levels of fundraising expertise.

1. **Nonprofit facts.** Learn key facts about your nonprofit. You should be able to talk comfortably about your programs, history, key financial information, the impact you're making, and any notable accomplishments and milestones. If you've built a marketing quiver, you have all the learning material you need.

2. **Storytelling.** Work on telling compelling stories: one that highlights why you're involved, one that shares an inspiring experience you or a beneficiary has had that shows the impact of the work you do, one that articulates your 30-second organizational overview, and one that makes a case why a donor should support you. Stories can inspire and motivate donors to give and get involved. The better you tell them, the more authentic and credible you become.

3. **Role-playing.** Learn and practice tactics for asking for donations and overcoming objections with team members and coworkers. This book is loaded with examples.

4. **Donor facts.** Learn as many interesting facts about your donors as possible. The more you know about your donors, the more receptive they will be to you and your ask.

5. **Go live.** Practice what you've learned on donors. Start small. Ask for non-monetary items first such as in-kind services or inviting donors to events. When you feel comfortable enough to ask for money, start by asking minor donors for modest donations. As your confidence builds, engage higher capacity donors and increase amount of the ask.

BUSINESS SERVICES
AND WORKSHOPS

Known in the industry as "The Rainmaker," Tom has helped thousands of organizations raise hundreds of millions of dollars. He will listen to your concerns and give your team the guidance and support it needs to achieve thundering fundraising results. Best of all, he'll do it at a price you can afford because he scales his fees based on ability to pay.

Tom also speaks regularly at conferences around the country, so if you're in need of a powerful, memorable, "edutainment" style retreat, workshop or speech, give him a call. Topics include:

- Getting board members wildly excited and engaged about helping support your fundraising efforts

- Rarely used key tactics to secure major gifts from major donors

- Let's have coffee! Winning face-to-face solicitation tactics

- Start smart! Build a high-impact strategic fundraising plan

- Frugal Fundraising! Raise BIG money on shoestring budget

- 7 ways to build a high-touch donor stewardship program

- Analyze this! Tactics to evaluate your fundraising programs/events

Looking for online tools?
Visit Tom's website. You'll find how-to video tutorials, podcasts, and dozens of strategies to help you become a fearless Rainmaker, create a winning fundraising program, build a thriving nonprofit, and live inspired.

Visit the site, become a fan, and he'll notify you of upcoming podcasts, videos, and interviews with industry experts. While you're there, check out Tom's bestselling book on nonprofit management and board engagement titled, *First Things First: A Leadership Guide to Building a Gold Standard Nonprofit (228pp)*. A must read for every board and staff member.

www.TomIselin.com

More praise for *Cloudburst*

"Tom has transformed real world experience into a seminal book every fundraiser and board member must read. He's simply brilliant."
Paula Isley, *Director of Development, inewsource.org*

"Tom delivers a clear and concise message for leadership with finesse! *Cloudburst* will be required reading and the fundraising inspiration for my boards."
Brigit Cavanagh, *Development Chair, Maine Motor Coach Network*

"This book definitely needs to be incorporated into every minister's seminary education. If you want to raise more money and care about stewarding your donors, study this book from cover to cover."
The Rev. Dr. Michael J. Spitters, *Lead Pastor of Expedition Church*

"Wow . . . I don't have enough words to express the excitement generated from reading *Cloudburst*. I now feel energized to take the lead on my fundraising committee. Thank you!"
Jeannette Davidson-Mayer, *R4 Alliance, Board of Directors*

"Tom provides a strategic platform packed with wisdom and experience for nonprofit leaders to build thriving fundraising programs."
Irma R. Muñoz, *President and Founder, Mujeres de la Tierra*

"Practical and easy to read. Looking forward to giving copies to all my board members."
Bill Fox, *Chairman, Grandparents as Parents*

"Easy to read cover-to-cover. Nothing lacking. Most books are dry and lose me. I recommend *First Things First*—it's a roadmap to nonprofit success!"
Carol Riza, *Executive Director, Bridge of Faith*